Growing Your Musician

A Practical Guide for Band and Orchestra Parents

Tony Bancroft

Published in partnership with
MENC: The National Association for Music Education
Frances S. Ponick, Executive Editor

ROWMAN & LITTLEFIELD EDUCATION
Lanham, Maryland • Toronto • Plymouth, UK

Published in partnership with
MENC: The National Association for Music Education

Published in the United States of America
by Rowman & Littlefield Education
A Division of Rowman & Littlefield Publishers, Inc.
A wholly owned subsidary of The Rowman & Littlefield Publishing Group, Inc.
4501 Forbes Boulevard, Suite 200, Lanham, Maryland 20706
www.rowmaneducation.com

Estover Road
Plymouth PL6 7PY
United Kingdom

British Library Cataloguing in Publication Information Available

Library of Congress Cataloging-in-Publication Data
Bancroft, Tony, 1969–
  Growing your musician : a practical guide for band and orchestra parents /
Tony Bancroft.
    p. cm.
  ISBN-13: 978-1-57886-599-4 (hardback : alk. paper)
  ISBN-10: 1-57886-599-9 (hardback : alk. paper)
  ISBN-13: 978-1-57886-600-7 (pbk. : alk. paper)
  ISBN-10: 1-57886-600-6 (pbk. : alk. paper)
   1. Music—Instruction and study—Parent participation. 2. Musical instruments—
Instruction and study. 3. Child musicians. 4. Practicing (Music) I. Title.
  MT1.B3135 2007
  784.4'4071—dc22   2006100809

∞™ The paper used in this publication meets the minimum requirements of
American National Standard for Information Sciences—Permanence of
Paper for Printed Library Materials, ANSI/NISO Z39.48-1992.
Manufactured in the United States of America.

Contents

Figures and Tables

FIGURES

TABLES

Foreword

Congratulations! You are most likely buying this book because you have a deep respect for your child and you want to see him or her improve and achieve his or her musical best. Music majors and professors can and should use this wonderful book, but it is not specifically designed for them. Rather, it is targeted for everyone with children in music.

As good as this book is, however, it should not take the place of a music director or a private teacher, nor should it be used as an end-all. It is a unique armchair-type book, and if used carefully it can produce splendid results.

This book is for musicians and their parents facing the long and challenging road toward learning and performing great music. It is for every parent and teacher, regardless of musical experience, who wants a shortcut to focused, high-level achievement. I've known many students who have started out strong in music only to hit a wall; it is perfectly suited for these musicians—and their folks, too! Mostly, though, this book is for anyone who wants to learn music and enjoy a lifetime of musical benefits.

My advice is to read the parts and chapters that are most appealing and useful to your unique situation. For example, if you already have an instrument to learn on, then skip most of part I, "Select the Right Instrument," and move on to part II, "Practice Makes Perfect." If you know little about music or perhaps never even played an instrument at all, consider shifting to the third part, "Secrets of the Pros." This will help acquaint you with the field at a comfortable pace. Afterward, you can consider jumping back to the other sections.

After reading this book, you will feel confident in knowing how to provide your musician with the very best opportunities for musical development. You will appreciate and recognize specific details about music. Perhaps you will also gain a unique understanding and deeper respect for the hard work and dedication that is required of a musician—and the great joy that music making can bring to a child and a family.

Congratulations for making the right choice to develop your musical child, and kudos to you for deciding to purchase this exceptional book. As a supplement to your local music program *and* your private music teacher, you won't find a better music resource.

Have fun!

Eyde Rugolo
Executive Director
Young Musicians Foundation
Beverly Hills, Calif.

Acknowledgments

Many people inspired, supported, and endured when I decided to take on the nearly impossible task of writing this book. Although I cannot thank all those who helped me, I want to name a few of them here.

First of all, thanks to all the people that made this book possible: my wonderful team at MENC: The National Association for Music Education —Frances Ponick and Ashley Opp. Thanks also to Paul Cacciato at Rowman & Littlefield Education and Moe Turrentine for his review and comments.

And on a more personal note, there are a few other people that I want to thank: my wonderful wife, Setsuko, who stood by and listened with open ears and fresh ideas throughout the entire development—*domo arigato*.

My loving parents, John and Jane, who raised me with a deep and abiding respect for education. They supported me long before this exciting book was conceived by providing me with access to essential private lessons from master teachers. Additionally, when I was young, they drove many thousands of miles just to expose me to higher levels of musical experience. Mom and Dad, you were there for my first concert, and you supported me all the way to Carnegie Hall. Thanks!

My terrific twin brother and fantastic best friend, John (and his wife Shiho), who after writing his own outstanding book, *They Call Me the Gambler—Betsumei Pachi Pro*, sparked the writing idea in me. John has encouraged me all the way from day one. You are truly an amazing and inspiring big brother!

My one-and-only favorite cousin, Emma, who plays the violin and loves soccer and basketball, and her parents, Aunt Barbara and Uncle Bret. My former teachers, colleagues, and students too numerous to name here in this brief space.

Additional thanks go to anonymous Ivy League alumni, Karen Calhoun, John Campbell, Marian Chiara, the R. D. Colburn School of Performing Arts, Don Doyle, Tom Duffy, Sue Edwards, Aaron Flagg, Steve Fraider, Frank Hauser, Monique High, Harry Leff, Katsuhiko and Fumiko Kanezawa, Jan King, Leah Komaiko, Julie Long, Pat Macki, Lorenn Marsteller, John Meyers, John Mosly, the Palos Verdes Library staff, Eyde Rugolo, Mike Seltzer, Helene Mirich-Spears, Dr. Frances Steiner, Joseph Thayer, Dr. Dan and Karen Webb, Akira Yodo, and Gill and Linda Zimmerman.

It seems only natural to dedicate this book to my wonderful grandma, Rose Bancroft, who inspired me in so many countless ways!

Introduction

$\mathcal{A}$s an educator, I have seen many of the young musicians I taught grow up to become wildly successful in diverse areas like music, sports, academics, and business. But not one child became a successful musician or an extraordinary adult without the involvement of his or her parents and other caring adults. As a general rule, the child with adult guidance, encouragement, and caring succeeds.

Playing a musical instrument can

- Help your child develop a commitment to excellence
- Help your child develop self-esteem
- Be an opportunity for your child to experience self-expression, creativity, and heightened achievement, as well as engage the imagination
- Be part of a balanced, positive, challenging, and stimulating education
- Prepare your child for other stages of development and participation in society by fostering dedication and sensitivity
- Increase your child's brain development, math abilities, and higher thinking skills
- Help your child develop perseverance when things are looking bleak and hopeless
- Raise your child's awareness
- Expand your child's knowledge
- Help your child develop mind and body coordination

- Contribute to your child's spiritual growth
- Help your child develop teamwork skills
- Be a source of great fun!

Parents and music directors need to be the guiding light and inspiration for beginning musicians. They must encourage and motivate them when things get rough and inspire them when things seem impossible.

But what if you want music for your child and you don't know anything about it? This book will tell you what you're getting into. You won't have to read music or try to learn more than your child does. What's important is that you are the parent of a unique individual, and you want to offer that individual the best opportunities available to succeed in life.

I'm assuming that you know practically nothing about music or music education. Even if you took music in school, the way music is taught these days is probably quite different from how you learned it. We go over three major areas—getting the instrument, practicing, and building skills. In the first part, I discuss buying versus renting an instrument, and I warn you about the pitfalls. The second part, "Practice Makes Perfect," has two chapters—one for you and one for your child. And I call the third part "Secrets of the Pros" because acquiring the skills described there is the first step beyond being an ordinary player.

You'll get the basics about being a band or orchestra parent here. No, I don't cover booster clubs or touring or chaperoning or contests. Those subjects are covered very well in other books that I list as resources. The main thing for now is obtaining a good instrument, helping your child figure out the best ways to practice, and learning how to listen and talk to your budding musician about music. I also discuss the National Standards for Music Education briefly. The national standards describe what children should know and be taught about music in words that anyone can understand.

I firmly believe that a commitment to learning how to play music with others contributes fundamentally to successful adulthood. The thousands of children I have taught have proven that to me. I invite you and your child to travel this fascinating and fulfilling road together.

I

SELECT THE RIGHT INSTRUMENT

• 1 •

Getting Started

My belief is that if you can talk, you can play.

—Kenney Werner, *Effortless Mastery:*
Liberating the Master Musician Within

MY TRUE STORY

$\mathscr{B}$efore scientific studies proved the positive relationships between music and brain development, my mother and father, two music-loving nonmusicians from upstate New York who could hardly explain the differences between "tone" and "intonation" or "staccato" and "legato," enthusiastically enrolled my twin brother and me in beginning band. We were eager eleven-year-olds and had no idea what to expect, but we wanted to learn how to play.

Like so many mothers and fathers in hometowns across America, somehow my parents intuitively understood the value of music. Like you, they recognized how aspects of music (practice and performance) are valuable and indeed play a crucial role in developing a child's focus, discipline, self-esteem, self-respect, and self-worth, not to mention musical skills. They also recognized that music is an end in itself; it is worth studying purely for its own merits. For these reasons and many others, my parents enthusiastically enrolled us in music.

The Journey Begins

Band was the class that all the cool kids signed up to take. Deep down inside, I knew music was going to be hard work, but I focused on the idea that music was going to be fun. Incidentally, I had heard that there was a chance that my group would go on a fun music trip to Disneyland. I would do anything to be a part of that.

The Challenge

My first week in beginning band was terrifying. It seemed that all the other kids already knew what instruments they wanted to play. To make matters worse, I thought they already had purchased brand-new instruments. As a tiny, quiet, eleven-year-old boy, what was I to do? As I looked around, I thought to myself, "Am I the only one without a shiny new instrument?" I tried to understand which instrument I should select.

I went home and asked my parents what they thought I should play. I specifically remember what they said: "We have no idea. What did your teacher say?" I asked a friend, and he said, "You should play the sax. It's cool!" Then my other friend said, "You should play the drums. They're cool!" I had no idea what to do. Heck, I just wanted to be in the group!

Finally I mustered up enough courage and approached Mr. Leff, my new band director. I asked him what he thought I should play. I'll never forget what he said. "Tony, you look like a brass player!" With his right hand, he gestured to the back of the room and said, "We don't have any tuba players in band. How about you try the tuba?" I had no idea what I was getting myself into, but I eagerly agreed to play anyway.

When I arrived home, I anxiously told my parents about my choice. Questions surfaced immediately. "How are you going to obtain a tuba?" "Where are you supposed to practice the tuba?" "How much does a tuba cost?" I was in a real pickle because I had no idea what a tuba even looked or sounded like! This is why "Select the Right Instrument" is the first part of this book.

The Result

Looking back, I see that very little serious thought was given to what instrument I should play. Luckily, I became an accomplished musician, graduating from some of the top universities in America while playing the tuba. Additionally, I have toured the world playing the tuba—not bad for a kid who had no idea what a tuba even looked or sounded like!

Because of my early, unnecessarily stressful experiences in music and my consequent development in and love for music, I've dedicated myself to eliminating stress and guesswork for you.

START OFF ON THE RIGHT FOOT

I'll never forget the advice my outstanding band director, John Mosly, used to give me: "There is nothing better than starting off on the right foot!" He actually meant the *left* foot because that is often how you lead off in marching band—but the point is to do what works and do it correctly. With that advice in mind, I can't think of a more appropriate point to start than the selection of an instrument.

And what about you? Are you starting off on the right foot? You decided to enroll your child in music because of the benefits music has to offer, right? But now what? Which instrument do you choose—string, woodwind, brass, or percussion? Should you buy an expensive instrument or rent? As soon as you answer one question, a host of others surface, each with its own areas of confusion and lasting consequences. The Q&A sections include some questions that can be answered right away.

Because music is a fun but complex art form, setting the proper foundation for long-term enjoyment, growth, and success is essential. Even before selecting an instrument with your child, it is wise to think about the future. Do you, like many parents, see your child as college bound? This may be one of the key factors influencing your decisions.

Involvement in music and the arts can have a great impact on your child's social and academic success. By being involved in a long-term intensive music program, your child will be more likely to enjoy a positive self-image, show empathy toward others, and achieve higher mathematics proficiency (yes, higher mathematics proficiency). In a study conducted by James S. Catterall, Richard Chapleau, and John Iwanaga, students consistently involved in instrumental music over a long period, compared to those not involved in instrumental music, perform better in math—18.1 percent better![1]

Many options (high vs. low, brass vs. woodwind, string vs. percussion, costly vs. inexpensive) will perplex even the experienced parent. It will seem even harder to select an instrument if you have little or no experience playing one. In a sense, you will be learning the ins and outs of the instrument along with your child. Take a look at the "Questions for Parents" quiz to help get you thinking.

Starting Off—Questions and Answers

What is the ideal age to start music?

Most school band and orchestra music programs begin in either elementary school (around ages eight to ten) or middle school (around ages eleven to thirteen). You should consider preparing your child *before* the first day of class begins.

What should we do in school?

If you are fortunate enough to have an elementary or middle school music program, consider starting your child first on an appropriately sized instrument. Some programs start elementary-age children only on recorders. Just keep in mind, whatever the instrument, that size does matter. Your child's body and hands are small, so select an instrument that he or she can hold properly. Your child's air capacity plays a very important role as well in determining which wind instrument to play. If your child is too small to blow properly into a full-sized or even student-sized wind instrument, the recorder may be the answer. In my opinion, recorders are ideal instruments for stepping up into a band instrument. Another option is to start your child on a string instrument.

What should we do if our school has no music program?

Consider enrolling your child in private music lessons. Piano has traditionally been the most popular instrument to learn because it typically serves as a gateway instrument to other instruments. And for those who truly enjoy playing music, the piano has unlimited possibilities. After all, a person can easily spend a good part of a lifetime learning, playing, and mastering the piano.

Questions for Parents

- Is your child interested in playing an instrument?
- Does the sound of the instrument inspire and motivate your child?
- Does your school music program have a band or orchestra . . . or both?
- Will your child need a brass, woodwind, percussion, or string instrument?
- Will the size of the instrument affect your child's decision?
- Will the size of your child affect your decision?
- If your child plays a large instrument, can you transport the instrument to and from school?

Your Child's Perspective

Many new musicians select an instrument because their friend plays a similar instrument. I call this the "cool" factor. Most kids think that if they play the instrument that their friend already plays, then they will be considered "cool." Keep in mind that most adolescents want to be part of the "in group." Because they want to feel popular and accepted, they are highly influenced by what their peers do (even when their peers make poor decisions). Selecting a "well-played" instrument is one way of feeling accepted by their peers, and this is "cool."

The Teacher's Perspective

Think about it. If everyone played the violin, there would be no orchestra. Likewise, if everyone played the clarinet, there would be no band! Although many music directors want your child to select an appropriate instrument, they also know that a large group of nothing but clarinet players does not constitute a well-balanced band. All music directors must carefully balance the perceived needs and desires of each student and parent with the needs of their ensembles.

Keep in mind that music directors must indeed push some instruments, regardless of child or parent desires. This is simply part of developing a well-balanced ensemble. In the long run, this serves the best overall interest of everyone.

Now, let's look at the steps you will need to take as you and your child try to choose the best instrument for you.

STEP ONE: TALK TO YOUR CHILD

Because there are so many different instruments—flute, oboe, clarinet, saxophone, trumpet, trombone, baritone horn/euphonium, French horn, tuba, violin, viola, cello, bass, and percussion—try to narrow down the choices. Focus on themes, for example, size (large vs. small) or pitch (high vs. low).

Another approach is to consider selecting or narrowing down instruments based on instrument groups (brass, woodwind, percussion, or strings), and focus on a specific instrument in that group. I've included a basic chart in this chapter that shows the four instrument groups and how instruments fit into them (table 1.1). This may seem like an overwhelming set of choices, but you should keep the big picture in mind and ask your child questions that will help him or her focus.

Talk directly about music with your child. An honest and straightforward conversation will go a long way to help your child focus his or her interests. Often an introduction with helpful and inquisitive questions is enough to focus a child. Listen intently to the answers, but be prepared: the answer you hear may not be the one that you were hoping for!

I've heard many stories from parents who want their children to learn the clarinet only to find out that their child really wants to play the drums.

Table 1.1.   Musical Instrument Groups

Sound	Brass	Woodwinds	Strings	Percussion
High Sound	Trumpet	Piccolo, Flute, Clarinet	Violin	Bells
Medium Sound	French Horn, Trombone	Alto Saxophone, Alto Clarinet Tenor Saxophone	Viola, Cello	Xylophone, Drums
Low Sound	Baritone Horn Tuba	Bass Clarinet, Baritone Saxophone	Bass	Bass Drum, Timpani

Be prepared for the possibility that your child may want to learn an instrument that is not ideal or practical for your family.

Bringing the subject up is a good idea, but it's best to explore further before the final commitment.

STEP TWO: EXPLORE MUSIC

Unless you are familiar with band and orchestra instruments, your next step will involve discovery. Seek out musical experiences in your community and enjoy this discovery period with your child. Attend live music concerts and events, and explore which sounds specifically appeal to your child and, by extension, which instrument he or she might like to play. Which sounds excite and inspire you and your child? The following strategies will help you and your child explore music.

Talk to Your Child's Music Director

You and your child have a lot to face when first starting band or orchestra, so let your music director help you get it accomplished in a timely, inexpensive, and low-stress manner. Your child's future music director will be delighted to know that you're interested in starting correctly. Your music director can save you time, money, and stress. He or she can answer key technical questions you might have and, more importantly, steer you in the right direction.

Your music director will know if an instrument is inappropriate or unreasonable. For example, children often think that they want to play the trumpet. A music director can easily assess if a child has the correct lips for successful trumpet playing.

Additionally, your music director can show you what you will need, what to expect, and how to go about renting or buying. Your music director may also be able to direct you to important live-music venues, local music stores, and other resources.

A Family Tradition

Jessica, a bright new student in middle school, arrived in music class not knowing exactly what to play. Like so many students, she was torn between the flute and the clarinet. Jessica thought both instruments looked petite and sounded pretty, but she was still unsure about which one to select. I suggested that she go home and discuss the differences between the instruments with her parents. Maybe she could come to a conclusion with her family's support.

The next day in class, when students were completing their instrument selection, Jessica beamed with pride as she handed me a note from her mother. The note read, "We decided that because her father played the clarinet, it will be best for Jessica to continue the family tradition on the clarinet." Jessica was very excited about carrying on this family tradition. Jessica's parents had helped her focus, and Jessica knew she had the support and encouragement of her family. She was now ready for the next big step.

Music directors are in an unusual position. Unlike some retail and sale positions, they don't work on commission, so they can usually speak honestly and openly about your needs and what you're getting involved with. Music directors are not trying to rip you off or give bad advice. While they do want to develop a balanced ensemble, they are also not likely to "force a sell" on you or pressure you into a poor decision.

Many schools supply instruments for free use. A few request a nominal fee. But because music directors are not involved in money-making ventures, you can expect valuable and useful advice.

Listen to Live Music

Recordings and videos are not bad, but it is important that you see the instrument live. A fun way to start thinking about music is to attend live concerts. The more you and your child are exposed to music, the more both of you will understand and relate to it. Listen to concerts at your school at every possible opportunity. Visit your local college and see a musical or opera performance. Sometimes a soloist in a local venue will be able to pique your interest in a particular instrument. The main idea here is to help your child make the best decision as to what instrument is the most appealing and appropriate.

While your family enjoys a concert together, have fun! Bring a picnic lunch if you can, but don't forget to ask your child the important questions: What sounds do you like? Which instruments look interesting? What do you think you would play if you were in the group? The answers to these questions will be of great value in the near future.

Visit Backstage

Unlike rock-and-roll concerts that often require a special backstage pass or press badge, band and orchestra concerts are usually open and accessible. Classical musicians are interested and usually eager to help families start out and succeed in music.

After a concert, see if you can walk backstage and talk with the musician who plays "your" instrument. Ask questions about how musicians get started and what it takes to be a successful musician. Give your child opportunities to engage in conversation. You will be amazed at how receptive, encouraging, and supportive musicians can be!

Hold and Play the Instruments

Some music programs provide short exploratory classes where all students get an opportunity to "test-drive" various instruments. In these exploratory programs, small groups of students and even entire classes have an opportunity to play and rotate through the primary instruments of band and orchestra. After a given time, the students may know which instruments they like and will be likely to select an instrument that is appropriate for them to learn.

Try the Family Exploratory Approach

Many schools do not have an in-house exploratory music program. Exploratory programs are frequently thought of as being too expensive. Additionally, there is often little or no time left in school schedules to include one. But all is not lost! As a parent, you can create your own homemade exploratory opportunity. This just involves a little bit of time—and it can be a lot of fun.

The family exploratory approach encourages parent involvement from day one. I am a firm believer that parents who are active and interested in their child's progress see their children succeed more often, not only in music, but in all areas of school. In fact, in a study reported in the *Journal of Research in Music Education*, parental involvement was found to be significantly related to emotional, cognitive, and performance outcomes. Students at all grade levels can benefit from increased parent involvement.[2] If parents actively help and guide their children from the beginning, their children are more likely to become successful in music and give music a serious shot, rather than just a halfhearted try.

A Story of Discovery

I was first introduced to musical instruments in the fourth grade. A teacher played all the instruments for us kids behind a large screen, and the trumpet or clarinet were the ones that sounded the best to my ears. Later, when I tried the clarinet, I couldn't get a sound out of it, but when I played the trumpet? *Bingo*—sound! I knew then that I wanted to be a professional trumpet player.

The sound of the trumpet somehow got stuck in my head. It struck a chord inside that was personal, and when I found out that I could play it, I was delighted.

—Bob Karon, Juilliard School graduate, master educator, and professional musician

---

Sometimes the best way to discover and learn something new is to do it your way! Creating an instrument exploratory experience from scratch may seem like a lot of work or even a waste of time. But it is a solid investment in your child's future. It will pay off in dividends for a lifetime; it will help your child's self-image and self-esteem; it will develop your child's confidence; it may even help your child in other areas like mathematics! For starters, try the ideas below:

- *Local School.* One of the best places to "test-drive" instruments is your local school. Many music directors have extra instruments that you can play or at least touch—for free. Music directors will sit down with you and your child, one-on-one, to demonstrate exactly how instruments work and what they sound like. This approach will help your child focus quickly and efficiently on an appropriate instrument. It also gives your child a tremendous amount of personalized attention and allows the teacher to help you efficiently analyze what instrument might work best for both you and your child.

- *Local Music Store.* Visit your local music store and ask to talk with a representative who is able and qualified to demonstrate instruments. Explain that you are in the process of choosing an instrument and ask for some brief introductory demonstrations. Many local music stores are in business primarily to help and support kids. Some music stores, hoping you will purchase an instrument from them, will demonstrate for free, showing you how to hold and play the instrument. Others may charge you a "lesson fee" for their time.
- *Word of Mouth.* People who are already in band or orchestra can easily tell you about instruments they like and how to become involved with one. This method can be very useful, but it does not give you an accurate picture of all the instruments. Most likely you will only learn one particular point of view, which can be limiting.
- *Reference Material.* Visit your local library. Use the Internet, or look in the *Encyclopaedia Britannica.* Here you will find pictures and descriptions of instruments. If you know a bit more about what you want to play, you can also look up the exact instrument under its specific heading. For computer-savvy folks, some good places to start looking and learning about instruments are at www.si.umich.edu/chico/instrument, www.datadragon.com/education/instruments, www.playmusic.org, and www.nyphilkids.org. A list of common band instruments is also available in appendix C.

STEP THREE: ANTICIPATE YOUR BIG DAY

Some children instinctively know what they want, but most do not. In fact, until you corner them into making a choice, many probably won't make one. Think of it like taking your child for ice cream. You need to familiarize your child first with the fact that you are going. Next, the store may have dozens of flavors, so you need to help your child get focused. The more your child knows before deciding, the easier it will be to make the correct choice.

Now you know that selecting the right instrument involves a lot more than window-shopping. I've included a checklist to help you organize your thoughts.

Checklist for Parents

- ❏ Plan to be actively involved in helping your child reach a good decision.
- ❏ Include your child in the discovery and selection process.
- ❏ Talk with your child about music.
- ❏ Decide which group of instruments piques your child's interest.
- ❏ Determine if your child likes high or low, big or small instruments.
- ❏ Learn about the different families of instruments (brass, woodwinds, strings, and percussion).
- ❏ Explore all instruments at school or at a local music store.
- ❏ Consult with your local music director.
- ❏ Take time to enjoy the learning and discovery process.
- ❏ Attend live music concerts.
- ❏ Go backstage at concerts and talk with professionals.
- ❏ Obtain as much information as possible about your options.
- ❏ Hold and play instruments before making your final decision.
- ❏ Be positive!

Thoughtful consideration and appropriate research will benefit you and your child. But what about the child who has exceptionally small hands? What instrument should he play? What about the child with an unusually pronounced overbite? Can she still play the trumpet? Then there is the question about children who can't sit still. What instruments should they play? Find out in chapter 2.

PARENTS: GO THE EXTRA MILE

- Attend a live music concert together.
- Consider private lessons for your child.
- Read about the history of a particular style of music or a famous musician together.
- After your child starts playing, put on special concerts for family, friends, and neighbors.
- Visit local music colleges just to look around.
- Encourage your child to join an after-school music program.
- Send your child to summer music camp.

NOTES

1. James S. Catterall, Richard Chapleau, and John Iwanaga, "Involvement in the Arts and Human Development: General Involvement and Intensive Involvement in Music and Theater Arts," in *Music Makes the Difference: Music, Brain Development, and Learning* (Reston, Va.: MENC, 2000), 74–101.

2. Stephen F. Zdzinski, "Parental Involvement, Selected Student Attributes, and Learning Outcomes in Instrumental Music," *Journal of Research in Music Education* 44, no. 1 (Spring 1996): 34–48.

· 2 ·

Tools for Selecting Your Perfect Instrument

Some people crave baseball. . . . I find this unfathomable, but
I can easily understand why a person could get excited about
playing the bassoon.

—Frank Zappa, quoted in
Germer and Germer, *Horning In*

$\mathcal{S}$electing an appropriate instrument does not necessarily mean helping
your child to select his or her favorite instrument. Consider selecting an instrument that matches your family's lifestyle, your living situation, and your
child's individual needs.

However, one of the most important factors to consider when selecting an instrument is the level of interest your child has in playing it. Without interest, it will be difficult for you or your music director to coach your
child. Additionally, it will be much harder to help a child "hang in there"
when the going gets tough (and it will get tough).

Body size is another key element to consider when selecting an instrument. You may not want to have your tiny daughter play the tuba—
she probably would not be able to lift this heavy instrument. Likewise,
you may not want to have a student with short arms play the trombone
—playing the low notes will be difficult because the player must stretch
to reach the outer slide positions. Additionally, a student with smaller
hands will probably not be able to properly press the keys or cover the
holes on a bassoon.

Other important considerations for parents include the *level of knowledge* that your musician may already have developed. For example, a child who has already studied piano may have a distinct advantage over a child who has had no previous musical training. He or she may already understand how to read musical notation (notes on a page) and internalize the beat (count) and may also have learned about rhythm and how to sustain a tone.

Previous musical experiences that may have helped your child build skills in *pitch differentiation* and *hand-eye coordination* can play a significant role in how you approach selecting a new instrument. If your musician has superior hand-eye coordination (from other, previous musical experiences), a developed sense of pitch (from performing regularly with the church choir), and high grades (from being talented, diligent, and persistent), then you may want to consider one of the two most challenging instruments—French horn or oboe.

Financial commitments are important to consider before selecting instruments. Even a small instrument like a flute can cost between two hundred and eight hundred dollars. A family under financial strain may not want to select a tuba (minimum cost: two thousand dollars).

Some students must walk to school, and they are required to carry all their school supplies and instruments with them. This may be problematic, especially for students with larger instruments. Can you imagine the weight of textbooks and supplies a young child must carry when walking to school—heavy science books, English books, math books, binders, pens, paper, supplies, *and* a musical instrument? Some schools don't have locker space or extra instruments for students to play, so a family may need to purchase two instruments—a practice instrument to be stored at home and another instrument for use exclusively at school. For other families, driving the student and instrument to and from school may be necessary, as walking would be impossible.

Another consideration: despite the excitement and positive motivation that result from starting to play an instrument, *sound*, especially sound produced by beginning band students, can be quite unpleasant to others. Instruments can be loud, and the sounds produced will carry long distances. If you live in close proximity to your neighbors, you may want to consider playing a "softer" instrument. A flute, clarinet, or violin might be ideal because they produce softer, smoother sounds and generally a relaxing tone. A saxophone or brass instrument could prove to be a very poor choice and lead to a negative experience.

A FEW WORDS ABOUT DRUMMING

When it comes to playing a new instrument, many children want to start on the drums. Drums are familiar to students because they appear in television, music, videos, and movies—everywhere. Many children can easily recognize and relate to drums because they are easy to distinguish by shape and sound—big and loud. For beginning students, drums represent a "cool" and familiar instrument, and this appeal makes them a popular first choice. Knowing this, don't be surprised if your son or daughter decides to be a drummer.

What many parents fail to realize until it is too late is that drums are very loud. Many households are ill-equipped to contain the intense noise and percussive sound, and, quite frankly, many neighbors do not appreciate the disturbance they create. If you do not have adequate practice space for the drums, it may be better to consider a different type of instrument.

Drum Stereotypes: The Total Percussionist

A few years ago, Steven joined the band and said he wanted to play the drums. Assuming that the drums were the easiest and the coolest instrument to play, he said he wanted to be a bass drum player because "it will be loud and easy." Steven was correct. Drums are fun (and they can be loud); however, Steven was missing the larger picture. He did not understand what is expected in order to become a complete percussionist and performer.

After I explained to Steven the concept of "the total percussionist" and told him that there is more to playing the drums than only learning to play the bass drum, Steven's eyes opened wide. He told me, "I want to learn the easiest instrument," not a large, complicated group of instruments.

Because there are so many instruments involved in playing percussion, playing the drums typically means that a drummer needs to be a more comprehensive music reader than the average musician. A drummer needs to become proficient in playing the entire set of percussion instruments. You don't just play the drums; you learn how to play the entire percussion ensemble—a huge (loud) challenge indeed!

Instead of just playing the bass drum, I suggested that Steven select an instrument he found interesting and wanted to become great at. "After all," I explained to Steven, "sounding good and being proud of your playing is the most important issue—not playing the easiest instrument."

Steven went home and spoke with his parents. He came to school later and said that he wanted to play the clarinet because it was small and sounded good. Eventually he played well enough to perform solos.

Few people truly comprehend how difficult it is to learn how to play all the percussion instruments. A person deciding to play the drums is not choosing one instrument, but many: snare drum, bass drum, timpani, suspended cymbals, crash cymbals, xylophone, bells, and auxiliary instruments like whistles, horns, buzzers, and triangles. If your child wants to be a drummer, introduce the concept of becoming a total percussionist and taking the responsibility to learn *all* the percussion instruments. Always demand rotation through instruments during practice, so that your child has the opportunity to become a master percussionist, not just a bass drum player—and your child will feel challenged and happy.

CUT THROUGH YOUR OPTIONS: THREE APPROACHES

Now that you understand some aspects of instrument selection, you will find detailed information below on logical approaches to selecting an instrument. These include a "Rate the Instrument" quiz, an Instrument Decision Matrix, and an Index of Difficulty chart. But remember that in the long run, mastery of an instrument has more to do with overcoming personal challenges and limitations than scoring a quiz. The quiz and corresponding tools should be used only as a general reference guide or starting point.

The "Rate the Instrument" Quiz

The "Rate the Instrument" quiz can make a difference. I have seen that children who have not been given this quiz tend to choose instruments more randomly and impulsively than those who have. Doing this quiz with your child should save you time, money, and frustration.

Once you have worked through the quiz, make a list of the top three instruments you selected and any additional comments that could affect your decision. If one is too expensive, not available, or for some other reason not appropriate, you still have two good alternatives to discuss and select from. Congratulations!

Step One: Study the Scorecard The scorecard, provided below (figure 2.1), is organized by columns and rows. The first column on the left lists instrument families (woodwind, brass, percussion, and string). Instrument choices are listed in the next column. Across the top are instrument characteristics. Black areas eliminate impossible or unlikely scenarios, so you should skip those. For example, a flute (a high instrument) will not be judged on low notes; therefore, you do not need to rate a flute on its low notes. Likewise, a tuba (a large, low-sounding instrument) will not be judged on its high notes. Here we go:

- Make two copies of the scorecard and an extra copy of the "Scoring Hints" section.
- Sit down with your child and explain how the scorecard works.
- Complete the quiz by following the instructions below, and ask your child to do the same.

Instrument Group	Instrument	Large	Small	Brass	Woodwind	String	Percussion	High	Low	Rhythmic	Melody	Bass	"Green" Instrument	Unique	Common	Heard Before	Recommended	Total
Woodwind	Piccolo																	
	Flute																	
	Oboe																	
	Bassoon																	
	Clarinet																	
	Alto Clarinet																	
	Bass Clarinet																	
	Alto Saxophone																	
	Tenor Saxophone																	
	Baritone Saxophone																	
Brass	Trumpet																	
	French Horn																	
	Trombone																	
	Baritone – Euphonium																	
	Tuba																	
Percussion	Percussion																	
String	Violin																	
	Viola																	
	Cello																	
	Bass																	

Figure 2.1. The "Rate the Instrument" Scorecard

Step Two: Take the Quiz   Fill in each box with a number (0, 1, 2, or 3). The higher the number, the more likely you are to select the instrument to play (0 equals no interest; 1 equals little or unsure; 2 equals possible interest; 3 equals definite or enthusiastic interest). Some categories may be of little importance to you or you may not be sure how you feel, so place a low score (1) in the box. When you come to a category that you find appealing and important, write in a higher number (2 or 3). If, for some reason, you have absolutely no interest in a characteristic, rate the category with a 0.

Scoring Hints

- Remember that 0 equals no interest, 1 equals little interest or unsure, 2 equals possible interest, and 3 equals definite or enthusiastic interest.
- Place the number from the rating scale that best expresses your feelings about each instrument characteristic in every available box in the column for that characteristic. For example, if your child is very small with short arms, you may want to put a 0 under large and a 3 under small. Read on for more information about each characteristic.
- In most cases, you will be putting the same number in every available box in a column. The only exceptions are the columns titled "Heard Before" and "Recommended" and the boxes next to "Percussion" in the "Large" and "Small" columns.
- *Large or Small.* This refers to the size of the instrument. Percussion instruments can accommodate children of any size, so put a 2 in both percussion boxes.
- *Brass, Woodwind, String, or Percussion.* Learn more about each of these instrument groups in appendix C. Place the appropriate number in every available box in each column.
- *High or Low.* This refers to the sound of the instrument. Some instruments, like the flute, have a very high sound, like a bird, while others have a low sound, like a foghorn. Decide how you feel about each type of sound and mark the columns appropriately.
- *Rhythm, Melody, Bass.* These characteristics are related to the type of music certain instruments typically play. Some just play rhythms, others play the melody (the main tune of the piece), and others provide a low bass line that complements the melody. Put the number that best indicates your feelings about each type of musical part in each column.

- *"Green" Instruments.* Colleges often offer hefty scholarships to students who play instruments that they are most in need of. Decide how important the possibility of such scholarship money is to you and mark the column accordingly.
- *Unique or Common.* Certain "unique" instruments are played by few students, while other, more common instruments are played by many students. Decide if you are interested in an instrument that stands out or one that lots of other kids play, and mark the columns.
- *Heard Before.* If you heard good things about a particular instrument (possibly from a television show or movie), mark how you feel about each instrument in this column.
- *Recommended.* If your music teacher has recommended playing or avoiding certain instruments, mark this column with the score that best matches your teacher's feelings.

Step Three: Tally the Scores   Calculate your total score for each instrument in the last column on the right. Share the results with each other. Make a list of the three instruments with the highest scores. Then combine your answers to find the best options for your future musical instrument. Include on your list any comments or additional information that could influence your decisions. You can write your scores on the Instrument Worksheet (table 2.1).

Instrument Decision Matrix

If you still have some concerns after taking the quiz and discussing the results together, use the Instrument Decision Matrix (figure 2.2) for further refining your instrument selection based on physical and emotional requirements.

Table 2.1.   Instrument Worksheet: Your Final Score and Ranking

Instrument Name	Total Score	Comment/Important Factor
#1 _____		
#2 _____		
#3 _____		
Example: Flute	30	I love the high sound!

How Does It Work?

- Read the section called "Eight More Factors for Refining Instrument Selection" below.
- Decide which factors apply to you and your child.
- Circle the X that applies to your choice on the Instrument Decision Matrix. For example, if you decide that you are interested in playing an instrument that uses significant quantities of air, go to the "Lung Capacity/Breath Support" column and circle all the Xs.
- After going across the matrix, count the circled Xs and write down the number in the right-hand column.
- Compare the number you wrote in the right-hand column with the total number possible in each row. If the two numbers are close, the instrument in that row could be a good choice for you!

Instrument Group	Instrument	Lung Capacity/ Breath Support	Hand/Arm Size	Body Size	Hand-Eye Coordination	Hand/Arm Length	Pitch Sensitivity	Rhythmic Sensitivity	Complex Fingerings	Total Number Possible	Total Number of Circles = Total Score
Woodwind	Piccolo				X				X	2	
	Flute	X			X				X	3	
	Oboe	X			X		X		X	4	
	Bassoon	X	X	X	X	X	X		X	7	
	Clarinet	X			X				X	3	
	Alto Clarinet	X	X		X				X	4	
	Bass Clarinet	X	X	X	X				X	5	
	Alto Saxophone	X			X				X	3	
	Tenor Saxophone	X	X	X	X				X	5	
	Baritone Saxophone	X	X	X	X				X	5	
Brass	Trumpet	X			X					2	
	French Horn	X	X	X	X		X			5	
	Trombone	X	X	X	X	X				5	
	Baritone – Euphonium	X		X	X					3	
	Tuba	X	X	X	X					4	
Percussion	Percussion				X			X		2	
String	Violin				X		X		X	3	
	Viola				X		X		X	3	
	Cello		X	X	X		X		X	5	
	Bass		X	X	X	X	X		X	6	

Figure 2.2. Instrument Decision Matrix

Eight More Factors for Refining Instrument Selection

1. Lung Capacity/Breath Support: the amount of air required. Woodwind and brass instruments use air; percussion and strings do not.
2. Hand/Arm Size: the size of the hand or arm. Some instruments, like the bassoon and tenor sax, may require a large hand.
3. Body Size: the size of the child's body. Some instruments, like the bassoon, bass clarinet, baritone sax, trombone, tuba, and bass, require a large body to play.
4. Hand-Eye Coordination: the extent to which the hand and eye will need to work together in order to play the instrument. Nearly all instruments require some degree of hand-eye coordination.
5. Hand/Arm Length: the physical length of the child's hand or arm. The tenor sax, baritone sax, trombone, cello, and bass require longer hands and arms.
6. Pitch Sensitivity: the degree to which a beginning player needs to be sensitive to varying degrees of sound. The oboe, bassoon, French horn, and all string instruments require a keen sense of pitch.
7. Rhythmic Sensitivity: the degree to which a beginning player needs to be sensitive to rhythm. Percussion instruments require playing of advanced and complex rhythms.
8. Complex Fingerings: the number of finger variations needed to produce a sound. Woodwind and string instruments have complex fingerings.

Making It Happen: There's Always a Way   Some children desperately want to play a certain instrument, even if it seems unsuitable. Here are a couple of examples of how to get around the problem.

Kathy, a beginning trombone student who was small for her age, had a tremendous problem reaching past the fourth position on her trombone slide. My first suggestion was for her to switch to the baritone horn (a baby tuba), but Kathy was determined to play the trombone, and she insisted that there must be a way for her to play (she is one of these children "born to play" the trombone). After doing some research, we found a product that could be attached to the instrument to help her reach the lower positions. The result is that Kathy can play smoothly from the closest to the farthest slide positions just like a long-armed trombone player!

Kevin, a beginning tuba student, had a huge problem. No matter how many telephone books and pillows we placed under him, he just couldn't safely reach the tuba and hold it properly. My first suggestion was to have Kevin switch to a smaller instrument like the baritone horn (baby tuba), which he could properly hold and reach. However, Kevin was born to play the tuba! He seemed to have his personal identity established as Kevin the Tubist. After carefully considering his options and knowing that buying a smaller instrument was out of the question (a new tuba costs at least two thousand dollars), we found a product that supported his tuba properly, allowing him to play correctly. Kevin's problem? Small body size. Kevin's solution? A tuba holder. Kevin ended up making honor band the next year—on tuba!

Index of Difficulty Chart

The Index of Difficulty chart (figure 2.3) will help you refine even further which instrument to play or not play by correlating instrument characteristics (listed as numbers 1 through 10) that your child will need to master. Instrument selection criteria are based on commonly accepted norms and my experiences; for example, it is commonly thought that it is very difficult to master pitch sensitivity on the French horn and oboe. That is why they are rated 10 in this category. Instruments with higher scores are theoretically "harder" to play and master. The last column yields an Index of Difficulty number. This number is the total from all the columns. In theory, the highest number correlates to the most difficult instrument.

Instrument	Lung Capacity/ Breath Support	Hand/Arm Size	Body Size	Hand-Eye Coordination	Hand/Arm Length	Pitch Sensitivity	Rhythmic Sensitivity	Number of Keys/Valves	Index of Difficulty
Flute	7	5	5	6	2	4	4	9	42
Oboe	9	5	5	9	2	10	5	9	54
Bassoon	6	8	6	9	8	9	4	10	60
Clarinet	4	5	5	6	3	4	4	9	40
Alto Clarinet	6	6	6	6	4	4	4	9	45
Bass Clarinet	8	7	7	6	5	4	4	9	50
Alto Saxophone	5	5	5	6	3	4	4	9	41
Tenor Saxophone	7	6	6	6	4	4	4	9	46
Baritone Saxophone	8	7	7	6	5	4	4	9	50
Trumpet	6	5	5	4	3	4	4	4	35
French Horn	7	7	6	5	5	10	4	5	49
Trombone	8	9	6	4	8	4	4	2	45
Baritone – Euphonium	8	8	6	4	4	4	4	4	42
Tuba	10	8	8	4	4	4	4	4	46
Percussion	4	4	Any	8	2	2	9	N/A	29
Violin–Viola	4	4	5	6	4	5	4	0	32
Cello	4	5	6	6	5	5	4	0	32
Bass	4	8	7	6	6	4	4	0	39

Figure 2.3.   Index of Difficulty Chart

You can use the Index of Difficulty chart in two ways:

1. You can compare it with your selections from the "Rate the Instrument" quiz or the Instrument Decision Matrix.
2. You can use the chart as your primary screening tool for an instrument.

Instructions
- Locate the instruments on the left side of the chart.
- Look at all the variables across the top and compare the level of difficulty (scaled from 1 to 10) in the corresponding box.

- Locate the overall total score (which is already filled in on the right side).

Examples
- If you know that your child has very short arms, likes high notes, and wants to play in band, you can match up the numbers in the chart and consider flute, alto sax, or percussion.
- If you know that your child is attracted to low notes and has long arms, you can match up the numbers and investigate baritone sax, trombone, tuba, or string bass.
- If you have two instruments that your child is equally interested in playing, you may find an insight that will help you make up your mind.

FREQUENTLY ASKED QUESTIONS AND ANSWERS

Listed in two groups below are the most common questions that parents and children ask about selecting a musical instrument. The answers provided will assist you further in fine-tuning and justifying your final instrument decision.

Questions from Parents

Should the music director review our decision before we buy or rent?
Yes. There may be unique or special circumstances that you are not aware of that may preclude your child from playing a certain instrument.

What if two or more instruments result in a tie?
There may be more than one instrument that appears to be a good match. For this reason, it is even more important for you to see, hear, hold, and try the instruments.

What if my child insists on learning an instrument that is not available for free at school?
You have three options—buy, rent, or borrow. Each option comes with its own advantages and disadvantages depending on your financial situation, your time horizon, and the availability of music stores in your area. Refer to the next chapter for more details.

What if my child has small hands, small arms, or a small body in general?

Depending on how small your child is, there are smaller student-sized instruments that can accommodate smaller hands and arms. Try flute, clarinet, alto saxophone, trumpet, violin, viola, or percussion.

My child is not especially coordinated. What should I do?

All instruments provide outstanding opportunities to develop and improve hand-eye coordination. Even a student with "poor" coordination can find an instrument. You may want to consider (or avoid) woodwinds and most brass instruments (finger coordination); trombone (slide-arm coordination); percussion (hand-eye coordination); and strings (finger and arm coordination).

What if my child has a difficult time recognizing pitch?

If your child has a difficult time hearing pitch, you may want to consider percussion. That said, however, percussion, like all instruments, does require some detailed pitch recognition. If pitch is a serious challenge for your child, even with extra help, stay away from the oboe, bassoon, and French horn.

What if my child just wants to play an instrument and be a part of a group?

If your child, like many, simply wants to participate and be a part of a larger group, ask your music director to see if there are openings for a particular instrument. Also, ask key questions that will help your child figure out what to play. Consider taking your child to hear professional groups perform to experience all the instruments. Questions relating to sound and style may help to identify a favorite.

What if my child is a "tapper" and constantly taps everything?

This may be a sign that he or she is born to play percussion. Some students are attracted to rhythm just as others are to tone and pitch.

What if my child absolutely refuses to play an instrument?

You should never force your child to play an instrument, especially if the child truly doesn't want to play. However, if you take your child to live music concerts, visit music stores to take introductory private lessons, and go backstage at important events, you should have no problem selecting at least one instrument that your child may be interested in learning to play. Keep in mind also that some kids like different types of music. It is also your job to help your child find the type of music in which he or she will find the most success.

What if my child is fascinated with the shape and color of an instrument?

Go with it if other factors, such as the size of the instrument, make sense. Children are fascinated with instruments for different reasons. Some prefer a certain sound and tone color, but shapes of instruments can also inspire a beginning musician.

What if my child wants to change instruments?

Wanting to try something new is a normal part of growing up. However, it is very important to become a "master" on at least one instrument. Self-esteem seems to go up as one becomes "good" on an instrument. If you must change instruments, consider doing it during summer vacation after a solid commitment of at least a year.

We just moved to a new school district, and the year is already half over. What if my child wants to start learning an instrument this late in the semester?

Your child will be much happier joining band or orchestra at the same time as everyone else. He or she will develop better social bonds as well as musical skills.

What if my child has braces?

Braces are a normal part of many child musicians' experiences. Although they may be uncomfortable, braces are generally not an impediment to learning an instrument. However, parents should be sensitive to the fact that most students feel discomfort for up to forty-eight hours after their braces are tightened or adjusted.

What should I do if my child has a hard time sticking with one thing and wants to change instruments after a few weeks or months?

For most students, it is very important to select an instrument and stick with it for at least one year. Losing interest, changing instruments, and not staying focused will have a negative impact on the quality of education that your child receives. Further, self-esteem may be difficult to develop without experiencing the results of consistent effort.

What if we can't afford an instrument?

When purchasing an instrument may be difficult or impossible, consider renting or borrowing an instrument from your local music store or school.

We live in an apartment. What instrument should my child play?

Although practicing an instrument every day doesn't seem like a problem to a young musician, a neighbor may strongly disagree. Try selecting an instrument that creates a softer, less penetrating sound, like flute, clarinet, violin, viola, cello, or bass. Stay away from loud, piercing instruments such as trumpet, trombone, French horn, and tuba. And be aware that drums make a tremendous amount of sound (your neighbors may even think it is noise).

My child walks to and from school every day. Which instrument is best for him?

Select a smaller, lighter instrument, like a flute, clarinet, violin, or trumpet.

I would like my child to earn a scholarship to study at college. Which instrument is the best choice?

Outstanding instrumentalists are rewarded financially by colleges every day. Grants and loans are available, usually by audition. Playing an instrument well increases your child's chances of earning scholarship money. Consider selecting a "green" instrument like those listed in appendix A.

My child can't sit still. What instrument should she play?

Music is a discipline that requires lengthy periods of focused concentration. If your child has a lot of trouble focusing, you may want to consult a school counselor or a medical professional. Talking privately with the music director ahead of time may also be helpful.

Questions from Children

What is the easiest instrument to play?

I hear this question every year, and it is difficult to answer. Theoretically, the bass drum is by far the easiest instrument to learn and play. But keep in mind that drummers must learn far more than just the bass drum; they should learn how to play all the percussion instruments. I encourage students to play melodic instruments like flute, clarinet, saxophone, trumpet, trombone, tuba, violin, cello, or bass. I usually start this way because it is quite easy for a musician who plays a melodic instrument to transfer existing skills to percussion instruments, but it is harder to transition from a percussion instrument to a melodic instrument.

What is the hardest instrument to play?

I also hear this question every year. The oboe, bassoon, French horn, and bass earn the highest scores on my Index of Difficulty scale; therefore, they all can be considered the most difficult to learn and play. Of these four, the oboe and the French horn are most likely to be the hardest. But these numbers may be off target depending on the strengths and weaknesses of a particular child. Remember, starting on the right-size instrument and having previous experience can have a dramatic impact on success. Things like hand and body size have a big impact on the difficulty of learning an instrument. I always tell my students that the hardest instrument is the one you do not want to play!

I want to play a certain instrument, but my teacher told me that I can't. What should I do?

There may be a very good reason why a professional suggests that you play one instrument and not another. Body size, expense, and availability are just some reasons why one instrument may be more appropriate than others. When starting out, find three instruments that you see yourself playing. If one is inappropriate for some reason, maybe one of the other two will be acceptable. Talk with your teacher or local music store for assistance.

How will I get a heavy instrument to school?

Carrying a heavy instrument to and from school can be the perfect reason for you to quit playing it! If you select a large or heavy instrument, you should find out if there is another instrument available for you to play at school. You do not want to carry a heavy instrument around all day. Perhaps having a locker or a storage area would help. If you walk to school every day, do not have a practice instrument at home, and can't rent an extra instrument, do not play a large instrument. Select a smaller one.

What if I don't like playing my instrument? Can I quit?

Students who learn music should make at least a one-year commitment. After all, it will take at least one year before you will begin to notice significant progress. The word "quit" carries negative implications, so I like to phrase it this way: music is not for everyone, but it is important to *try* music. If, after giving yourself a fair shot at learning a new instrument, you still think music is not for you, then learn another skill where you will find greater success and happiness.

What will my friends think if I play in the band or orchestra?

Peer pressure can lead to anxiety and poor decisions. It is important to discuss band and orchestra with your parents. You'll need their support. Learning an instrument won't always be fun and cool. There may be times when it's hard to continue because not everyone will be doing it, but dealing with these issues is a normal part of growing up. Be proud of your unique accomplishments and skills. It's not easy to play an instrument. Learning how to do it is worthy of considerable praise and celebration.

STILL NOT SURE?

If you and your child don't know or don't care what he or she plays, but still your child wants to be a part of the group, ask your music director or teacher for help.

Music Review Checklist

- ❑ Take the "Rate the Instrument" quiz and learn about the different instruments and instrument characteristics before actually selecting an instrument to play.
- ❑ Put yourself in your child's position in order to understand why he or she wants to play a specific instrument.
- ❑ Consider important characteristics including likes, dislikes, and physical requirements before selecting an instrument.
- ❑ Take some time each day to enjoy the learning and discovery process.
- ❑ Use the Instrument Decision Matrix and Index of Difficulty chart to confirm which instrument is most appropriate for you and your child.
- ❑ Consider your living environment in order to see if your instrument selection is appropriate.
- ❑ Consider the differences between a drummer and a "total percussionist."

❑ Understand that your child will need to make at least a one-year commitment (preferably two or three) in order to get a fair shot at learning some basic musical skills.

❑ Have fun.

Purchasing an expensive instrument seems like a gamble, doesn't it? What if you purchase an expensive instrument and your child suddenly wants to quit? Every parent must face these questions and others, including, Will I actually save money if I buy, or would I be better off renting? In the next chapter, budget-minded and dollar-wise families will find useful information to help them decide which route to take.

· 3 ·

Buying and Renting Instruments: What to Expect

Music produces a kind of pleasure that human nature cannot do without.

—Confucius, *Book of Rites*

Selecting and purchasing or renting an instrument can be very exciting. Even so, you may feel some apprehension. You may be worried about the financial commitment involved in purchasing the instrument; after all, instruments can cost over a thousand dollars. Additionally, a lack of knowledge about a new instrument could put you in the position of not knowing how to ask the right types of questions. Finally, you may feel insecure about acquiring an instrument that your young musician may not even like to play, and may want to give up on after a short time. Rest assured that a good experience awaits the vast majority of families!

Although there may be some great "bargains" available at pawnshops, discount stores, and Internet sites, be careful. Sometimes a deal is just too good to be true. The instrument you may be interested in always looks (and sounds) better in front of a salesperson. Don't get too caught up in the hype of the sale. Focus on obtaining a good-quality instrument.

I have seen students obtain great instruments at fantastic prices from the Internet. But regardless of its origin, when the instrument breaks or needs basic servicing (and with a young musician playing, it often does), you still need to take it in for service at your local music store. Cleaning and repairing can cost a lot, especially since your instrument will most likely not be under warranty if you buy it online. If you do insist on shopping online, have a professional examine and play the instrument before you purchase it. Unfortunately, I have seen students and parents get ripped off on the Internet. Don't be one of them!

Music stores are very sophisticated about product inventory and display. Consequently, you can expect to see many instruments and supplies when you enter a store. You may find it is difficult to comprehend the full range during one visit. Indeed, you may feel overwhelmed! If you remain focused, you are likely to end up with what you want rather than with something you don't really want or need.

By far, most parents' biggest concern is money. While it may be possible to find an instrument for a few hundred dollars or even less, depending upon the circumstances, I tell most parents that they are going to need to invest about a thousand dollars during the first year. Parents need to obtain an instrument, music, a music stand, and, depending upon the instrument, a host of other nickel-and-dime items.

The biggest decision you as a music parent will have to make is whether to buy a new, expensive instrument or rent or lease an instrument. Sometimes, buying an instrument for a child says "I know you will succeed!" Looking your child straight in the eye and saying that with confidence feels great. But renting an instrument can also make a difference in your child's world. You are giving your child a chance to learn an instrument, and by doing so, you are promoting important values, including teamwork, persistence, and empathy for others. Renting an instrument for your child can be one of the best things you will ever do.

However, children can misinterpret messages you send. By renting an instrument, you may be unintentionally sending the message that it's OK to try something new, but that if it isn't going well, there's an easy way out. Your child may believe that after trying the instrument for a while, he or she can always switch to another instrument or quit completely.

In the end, rental or purchase decisions can be complicated by a child's emotions and a parent's financial realities. I recommend that you make your decisions with great consideration and respect for the long-term development of your child. Some factors that you should consider are discussed below.

LEVELS OF QUALITY

Depending upon the circumstances (used, new, free, or rental) you can find instruments at your school (talk to the music director), at the local music store, on the Internet, or in your local newspaper. You might also check with family and friends to see if they have an instrument they no longer use. All of these sources are discussed below.

Band and orchestra instruments have various purposes and associated levels of quality. You should also give some thought to what level of quality you are looking for. Here are brief descriptions of the various levels:

Entry Level

If you are unsure about your child's interest in music, if you don't know if he or she will like it, or if you simply are "testing the waters," then start at this level.

Middle Level

For those families that know what they want and need, and for students who are serious about developing and reaching the next level in music, this is the place to begin. I suggest most families start here if possible. The instruments in this category are typically of a higher quality and allow your child to grow more than an entry-level instrument. If you start on an entry-level instrument, you may find that after a short while you will need to jump up to the middle level anyway, which may be costly.

Advanced Level

This level is for the serious musician. If you know that your child is "born to play" an instrument, or if you know that he or she has tremendous talent, ability, and drive, this is the right level for you. Typically, a serious music student or someone planning on playing in college and beyond will strive to own this level of instrument.

Regardless of the level of instrument you choose, there are a few basic questions that apply to any instrument to be purchased. Use the Quality Quiz to see if yours is up to snuff. If you're not happy with the answers you get, don't buy the instrument from that vendor.

Quality Quiz

1. If my child doesn't take to the instrument, can I exchange it for another instrument or receive a full refund? _____ Yes   _____ No
2. Do you have a rental program? _____ Yes   _____ No
   If so, how does it work?
3. If we rent, does the money that we spend go toward the purchase of the instrument? _____ Yes   _____ No
4. Does the instrument come with a case? _____ Yes   _____ No
5. What are the extra parts or pieces that I need to purchase in order for the instrument to work properly?
6. What if the instrument breaks? Is there a warranty? _____ Yes _____ No
7. Can this instrument be repaired by you or a third party you can identify? _____ Yes   _____ No
8. Are repair parts standard in the industry and easily obtained? _____ Yes   _____ No
9. How long does it normally take to repair this type of instrument?
10. Can we change an instrument before the rental period is up for a different instrument of the same type or a completely different instrument (e.g., upgrade the instrument, or switch from violin to clarinet)? _____ Yes   _____ No
11. If the music teacher evaluates this instrument and thinks it is inappropriate for my child, will you take it back? _____ Yes _____ No

OBTAINING THE INSTRUMENT

Most music stores accept credit cards. They may or may not ask for a cash deposit on the instrument, but you can count on showing a credit card to secure use of your rental instrument. Also, expect to provide deposit money for a cleaning and repair fee, which will be used to service the

Table 3.1.   Buying vs. Renting

Month	Purchase Outright	Rent-to-Own	Rent-to-Return
1	$1,000	$300	$200
2	—	$100	$150
3	—	$100	$150
4	—	$100	$150
5	—	$100	$150
6	—	$100	$150
7	—	$100	$150
8	—	$100	$150
9	—	$100	$150
10	—	—	$150
Totals	$1,000	$1,100	$1,550

instrument after it has been returned. As you can see in table 3.1, there are financial tradeoffs between buying and renting. These are addressed as part of the four basic options discussed below. The table assumes that your instrument costs $1,000 and that the time period for payments (if you choose that option) is similar to the traditional ten-month school year.

Option 1: Get a Free Instrument

Acquire a free instrument from your school, or borrow one from family or friends. The cheapest way to acquire an instrument is to get it for free!

Instrument selection at school is usually pretty straightforward. The earlier you select the instrument, the better off you usually are. A good group needs a mixture of musicians on various instruments. Therefore, those who choose first usually have an advantage; they get to play exactly what they want to play. At many schools, the process works like this:

1. The music director demonstrates instruments.
2. Students focus on an instrument group or a specific instrument that they are interested in learning.
3. Students select the exact instruments that they want to play and are placed in the appropriate group.

There are several advantages to selecting an instrument before the first day of class. Unlike the student who waits or is unsure, the decisive student can select the most desirable instrument instead of the one that's left after the other students have chosen. Also, because the school may have newly purchased instruments ready to check out, an early bird may be able to check out an instrument for free. Meanwhile, the other students and their parents will still be trying to figure out what to do.

Borrowing an instrument is also free, but a child who learns on an instrument borrowed from a friend or family member must be prepared to be at least as responsible for it as he or she would be for a school-supplied instrument.

If You Love It, Don't Leave It: Anna the Flutist   Anna was a bright, bubbly flute player who acquired her instrument from a trusting neighbor who played many years ago. Anna played every day, and after school before walking home she would pick her flute up and put it in her backpack, where it fit perfectly. Eager to learn and improve, she always practiced (a music director's model student).

One day Anna forgot her instrument outside the school cafeteria. By the time she and her mother realized that it was missing, they returned to school only to find it was indeed gone. Can you imagine the sheer panic Anna and her mother must have felt?

We looked at school and placed advertisements in all the local papers, but to no avail. The flute was gone for good, and somehow Anna had to explain to her neighbor how she had lost it.

Borrowing a free instrument from your school has its advantages, but most families don't have the luxury of obtaining a free instrument. What about renting versus buying? Which one is cheaper? Which one offers you the most flexibility? Which one is the right choice?

Option 2: Rent-to-Return

The rent-to-return option offers the most flexibility but also costs more in the long run. With this method, you rent an instrument, and if after a given time period (usually sixty or ninety days) you decide to walk away from the instrument, there is no penalty. Keep in mind that you do not keep the instrument, nor do you get any money back. This method allows you tremendous flexibility because you are not "stuck" with an instrument. However, as you can see from table 3.1, even in one year you are likely to pay significantly more for this method than for the other methods. The advantages are extreme flexibility and comparatively low monthly costs. But you do not own the instrument, and payments made do not go toward the purchase of your next instrument. There are also deposits and cleaning fees associated with this method.

Option 3: Rent-to-Own

The next option is renting to own. When you rent to own, all or most of the money you pay for the rental is applied to your eventual purchase. This is a very economical method, especially if you cannot afford to purchase the instrument all at once. And it is a good choice if you must rent because it typically does not cost much more than paying in full, yet it leaves you with some flexibility if you need to change instruments.

There are several more advantages to this method. You can make low payments over time (often interest free), and all payments go toward purchasing the instrument. If your child decides to play a different instrument, then you can usually apply the total amount already paid toward the new instrument. Dealers usually charge a small administration fee for this method, but as you can see in table 3.1, it costs only a few more dollars than an immediate purchase. The disadvantage of this method is that it may encourage you and your musician to "shop around" and try other instruments instead of digging in and learning the instrument you carefully select. (Consider this: for some kids, knowing that they can quit or change instruments gives them a good reason to do just that.)

Option 4: Buy an Instrument

In the long run, paying for an instrument in full on day one or on a no-interest payment plan if you can get one is usually less expensive than renting. The advantage is that you own the instrument and pay no interest or fees. The disadvantage is that if your child decides to quit or doesn't like his or her choice, you are stuck with the instrument. Few music stores "trade back" instruments.

In my opinion, it is in your best long-term financial interest to own an instrument, and it is in your child's interest to have a good-quality instrument. Although music stores have the potential to make a tremendous amount of money on rentals, most stores prefer to sell new instruments rather than rent used ones. They respect the need to start a musician on a good-quality instrument. They also understand that older instruments have more problems and need more repairs—a lot more, and this is inconvenient for you, them, and especially your child.

The Internet and local newspapers are also very good places to look for instruments. If you decide to shop around, you can use the Music Store Comparison Form (table 3.2) to keep track of instrument models and prices. Regardless of where you look, however, use the Quality Quiz. The most important question on the quiz is "If the music teacher evaluates this instrument and thinks it is inappropriate for my child, will you take it back?"

Then use the Instrument Purchase/Rental Checklist and go for your own perfect score!

Instrument Purchase/Rental Checklist

- ❏ We have decided on an instrument.
- ❏ We have committed to at least one year of learning the instrument.
- ❏ We have considered the student's and local music teacher's perspectives.
- ❏ We have decided whether buying or renting is our best option.
- ❏ We are satisfied that we obtained a good-quality entry-level or mid-level instrument.
- ❏ The instrument comes with a case.
- ❏ We purchased extra materials (for example, reeds, sticks, strings).
- ❏ We purchased a music stand.

Table 3.2. Music Store Comparison Form

Store Name	Make-Model	Number	Cost	Specifications
Example: Allegro Sales	Ferlo-315	335	$450	Silver with reeds and case

❑ We purchased a method/study book.

❑ We purchased a fun book (for example, a solo book).

❑ We reviewed the warranty and know when to service the instrument.

❑ We are confident that we know the process and have made informed choices.

Key Shopping Points—Music Store Questions and Answers

There are important questions to ask while shopping at a music store. While every transaction is a little different from the next, the questions listed below will assist you with your transaction.

Is the instrument new or used?

A used instrument should cost considerably less than a new one—at least 30 percent less. If the instrument you are considering is used or if it was previously rented to another person, check to find out if it works correctly. Make sure there are no cosmetic flaws or imperfections. If there are moving parts, make sure that they move correctly.

Is there a warranty? For how long? What does it cover?

All new instruments should come with a warranty at no extra charge. Many used instruments also come with a warranty. If you purchase your instrument from a reputable dealer, you can expect them to stand behind their product and, in case of problems within at least the first thirty days, repair or replace the instrument (assuming normal use).

What type of repair and service policy is offered?

Many instrument stores will repair or replace an instrument during the first thirty days of use. Many stores will also perform a "tune-up" or "servicing" on the instrument. A tune-up can involve adjusting pads and springs, cleaning, and other maintenance tasks.

Is the instrument a standard color, shape, and size?

You want to be extra careful here! Instruments come in student sizes and professional sizes. It is very important to purchase the correct size instrument for your child. If you have a small child, you will want to carefully review the instrument while your child is holding and playing it.

Some instruments also come in various colors and keys. Ask for the standard-size instrument.

Do we need to purchase extra equipment, accessories, or other special materials?

Most instruments come with a case but require extra materials that are not usually included. Do not expect music stores to include extra strings, reeds, or music. You will need to purchase these items separately. Refer to appendix C for required instrument material specifications.

How long should my child's instrument last before it needs to be repaired or replaced?

If your child takes good care of the instrument and does not abuse it, then the student-model instrument should last for at least two to three years. If your child is serious about playing music, you can expect to have an entry-level instrument for only two years or until your child physically outgrows it.

What is the resale value of my child's instrument after one to three years?

Resale value can vary greatly, depending on the instrument and its condition. If your child takes good care of the instrument, you can expect to recoup about half of its original cost.

My child has a quality instrument. What else does he need to be successful?

Many instruments require additional accessories, such as strings or reeds. Refer to appendix C and look up your child's instrument for specific information. Your child will also need a tuner, a metronome, and music books.

What is a tuner, and why does my child need one?

A tuner is a small electronic device that measures sound frequency. It helps a musician learn exactly where his or her instrument plays in tune. Learning how to play exactly in tune can take years, so a tuner can help focus and streamline the learning process. A tuner should be in every advanced musician's practice room.

What is a metronome, and why does my child need one?

A metronome is a device that tracks and clicks time, like a clock or watch. Your clock or watch clicks out seconds sixty times a minute, which is exactly what a metronome does. The big difference is that the number of metronome clicks per minute can be increased or decreased to accommodate the different speeds of music. All advanced musicians should own a metronome. Your child can slow down the time on the metronome to practice a piece in "slow motion." When ready, your child can speed up.

Should we purchase a tuner and metronome now or later?

You should purchase both a tuner and a metronome within the first six months of learning to play.

Should we purchase a music stand now or later?

A music stand is very important for your child's success. You should purchase a music stand immediately after purchasing the instrument.

What types of music books should I purchase?

Everyone in music wants to have fun and improve. The goal is to be able to play and sound great. But what type of music should your child study and learn in order to reach that goal? There are so many music books on the market that it may seem difficult to select the correct one. Visit your local music store, but don't become overwhelmed by the number of options. Most stores are organized in sections containing headings like *Brass, Woodwinds, Strings,* and *Percussion.* Many also have separate sections for piano music, rock music, and vocal music. Other stores may be organized by teaching category: band or orchestra. Simply find the appropriate section for your child's instrument. The following are examples of some of the types of books you should consider.

Method Books   Most schools use special books called method books. Think of these books as academic textbooks. They come in three major categories—beginning, intermediate, and advanced—and they often cover important skills required in order to learn how to play an instrument. They include basic music reading, fingerings, drills, and performance pieces. Many of the newer books come with compact disc recordings as well.

Developmental Books   Think of these books as private lesson texts. Not quite a musical textbook or a method book, developmental books help children move forward to the next level. They resemble method books in that they can be more academic than real music. They are primarily used in addition to method books and are popular with private teachers and their students. Most teachers use them exclusively when teaching privately.

Solo and Chamber Music   Would your child rather play a piece in the style of Mozart or play a piece written by Mozart? Solo and chamber music encapsulate some of the most challenging music available! Often the most challenging and yet the most fun are the "solo" and "chamber music" collections, and there are literally thousands of these songs available. These songs can be used to develop and hone musical skills even further than the method or developmental books. Plus, they are "real" music; therefore, they are inherently more fun (and arguably more challenging) to play.

Fun Music   There is also a different class of music that I call "fun music" because it is not really designed for learning or developing. It is simply designed to play for fun. Collections of popular movie songs, country music, rock and roll, musicals, and seasonal or religious music are collected in medley-style books. Your child can turn on the compact disc accompaniment and play along with the prerecorded rock band or orchestra. It's a lot of fun!

II

PRACTICE MAKES PERFECT

· 4 ·

What Is Practice?

Take passages apart like a jigsaw puzzle.

—Mike Seltzer, trombonist and teacher

THE JOURNEY BEGINS

*W*hen I was starting out in music, I remember how difficult it was to practice and improve. My music director insisted on regular practice, but like many musicians, I just didn't understand what I was supposed to do. I had thirty minutes in a room by myself. How in the world was I supposed to structure my time?

Probably the most challenging obstacle you and your child will face is not how to produce a tone, press a button, or count a rhythm; rather, it will be learning how to improve. In music, careful analysis, introspection, and repetition are called *practice*—and it is not easy to master.

Practice isn't easy, and without special training, good practice is almost impossible. I know very few professionals who actually enjoy it. How many people enjoy closing themselves in a room and diligently working on things that they aren't proficient at or may never be able to do perfectly? Not many! And I don't blame them.

Positive words of encouragement from parents and teachers frequently inspired me to achieve great things! You should make positive comments daily about your child's practice efforts. You'll be inspiring your child to work hard, never give up, and maintain high standards. If your child is encouraged correctly, learning music will become a fun personal challenge, not a tedious, drawn-out nightmare.

In my work with thousands of musicians, I find two main reasons why musicians do not achieve great success in music. The first is lack of practice, and the second is lack of knowledge about what to practice.

When I ask young musicians about their challenges in practicing, they often share similar types of problems. Here is what they say about what makes practice so difficult.

- "It's difficult to figure out exactly what to practice."
- "It's hard to know what I need to learn when I practice."
- "It's hard to be your own teacher—you need a special coach or private teacher to help you."
- "It's done by yourself, so you need to be motivated. Lack of energy is usually my biggest problem—once I get started I keep rolling along."
- "Sometimes I just don't feel like practicing and there seems to be no time left in the day."

WHAT PRACTICE *ISN'T*

People do not intrinsically know how to practice. Yet most music directors and parents wish that their musicians spent more time practicing. Music directors insist that practice is vital to development, and parents believe that daily routine is valuable. But a number of music directors and many parents can't explain exactly how to practice.

Just sitting down to play music is not practice. It may be fun and rewarding, and it may fulfill an important need for expression, but it is not practice. Did you know that all professional musicians use concrete techniques in order to practice well? And all professionals will tell you that practice is not always fun. Practice requires analyzing parts, organizing priorities, creating action plans, making assumptions, reacting to realities and limitations, and reviewing music over and over until it can be performed correctly, or at least as well as possible. Successful musicianship requires regular practice, and practice should *never* be used as punishment.

Young musicians frequently mistake the conventions of music practice with those of music performance. They sit down, play their music from beginning to end, and are done—and they think this is practice. An important distinction between practice and performance is that practice divides the whole into smaller parts. Performance is the whole—the entire piece straight through from start to finish. Practice is preparing the smaller parts for the performance. It is a means of eventually achieving the whole, which is greater than the sum of its parts.

Many musicians do not realize that they are wasting a tremendous amount of time and energy by playing straight through. As they try to improve, they repeat the same mistakes over and over, needlessly playing the parts they already perform well and wastefully playing over the parts they missed earlier. The mistakes that they are hoping to fix are eventually repeated so many times that they become ingrained—and very difficult to correct. The music seems harder than it really is.

This "straight through" approach, what I call passive practice, can be thought of as merely glossing over the surface details of music. Passive practice is playing music with little or no regard for important musical elements like notes, rhythms, phrasing, or style; making few, if any, corrections; and ignoring technique, meaning, and interpretation. People use this linear technique because that is how they typically do things like reading books or riding a bike from point A to point B—from start to finish. Using similar linear methods in practicing music, they try their best and either get it right or don't—but often they don't. This is why passive practice is not a good technique!

WHAT IS ACTIVE PRACTICE?

Active practice encourages musicians to make decisions before even playing a note. These decisions can relate to technique, phrasing, meaning, interpretation, and style. With the active-practice method, students approach music like a large puzzle that they dissect, interpret, reassemble, and demonstrate. When done correctly, active practice can be applied to nearly any piece of music. This method of music mastery ultimately leads to great musicianship.

A musician who practices using active-practice techniques demonstrates an increased awareness of the parts that make up the whole and a heightened sensitivity to musical sections that need more work. Musicians who use active-practice techniques stop and spend time on difficult passages, learning them before moving on. By learning the individual parts well, they are able to thoroughly master the whole. Children using active-practice techniques will mark the challenging sections in the music with a pencil and move back and forth through the music, isolating the difficult parts and playing them again and again until they are perfect. Active practice requires three essential elements: organization, purpose, and discipline.

Organization

Active practice requires organization. Your child must have all the required materials for practice (an instrument, music, a well-lit room, a chair, a music stand, a pencil, etc.) as well as good time-management skills.

Purpose

Musicians should practice with a distinct goal—a vision of where they are and where they want to be. Your child will learn to see music in a whole new way. This increased sensitivity will make your child much more aware of the challenges that must be overcome in order to perfect music.

Discipline

It is not easy for a musician to dissect a piece of music or figure out what he or she currently cannot play well but needs to learn. Knowing how to tackle difficult music and then doing it requires discipline.

Chapter 5 will further explore active-practice techniques with more specific information for your musician about what exactly to do during a practice session.

PLAYING MUSIC IS HARD WORK

For many, starting off in music seems easy enough. They learn a few notes, maybe even a few pieces, but frustration can set in when it comes time to jump up to the next level. What many kids start to think when they face their first serious hurdle is that they could be doing a host of other "important" things like watching television or playing video games. Many children see that learning new music means more work, and why would they want to do that?

It is important for you and your musician to understand from the first day that playing an instrument requires patience and hard work. Success should be clearly defined in terms of long-term and short-term goals. For example, learning a note is a short-term goal. Learning a whole scale is a medium or even long-term goal. Being accepted into an advanced music group is a long-term goal. Avoid unrealistic expectations about the "easiness" of a particular instrument or the time required to practice and improve. Ultimately, musical success requires respect, responsibility, dedication, and, most of all, disciplined, hard work.

SELF-CONFIDENCE: A BENEFIT OF PRACTICE

In addition to reviewing and strengthening musical skills and knowledge, practice serves to hone technical and mental skills. A by-product of practicing is consistency, and as that develops, self-confidence goes up as well.

If you want to become good at hitting a ball, you must go to a batting cage and practice batting. At first it may be hard, but gradually, the more balls you hit, the more confidence you gain. As your confidence increases, you feel better. You predict that you will be able to hit the next ball. This positive cycle feeds on itself, and as success becomes inevitable, you start to have more fun.

Similarly, a child who wants to learn how to ride a bike needs to get out on the road and practice riding. At first, he or she may be scared or get hurt by falling over, but by practicing, the child will gradually gain more skill and confidence (and fewer bruises). Eventually, this confident bicyclist will glide down the road with a big smile.

Music works the same way. Good practice habits encourage self-confidence and foster pride. Practice opens up a world of musical possibilities and enables dreams and expression to flourish. What makes practicing music unique? Unlike hitting a ball or riding a bicycle, music skills take longer to develop and more energy to refine because of their unique mental and physical challenges. By mastering these skills and learning to play the right notes at the right times with consistency, your child will increasingly gain self-confidence.

Further, musicians who learn and master their musical instruments and improve themselves, not necessarily for their own personal gain but for the good of their larger group, are truly an asset to our society. These are the people many of us want to be around and work with in our everyday lives, and they are the people businesses and community organizations hope to attract. Careful development of these important people is a worthy goal. And, believe it or not, learning to play a musical instrument and all that it entails—including practice—can help your child develop into such a person. Identifying obstacles and overcoming them—which lies at the root of practice—is one of the key qualities of outstanding character. Musical development will indeed help build character.

SET YOUR CHILD UP FOR SUCCESS

There are two primary needs all musicians have: physical needs and psychological needs. Mental energy and emotional support are as important as physical things like a music stand. After all, if you can't think about, focus on, and care about a musical goal or concept, then surely you won't be able to learn it! Review the Musician Needs Checklist for physical and psychological needs, and see if your child has everything required to be successful.

Mark a check next to each physical or mental component that your child already has. If your musician is lacking in any area, think about how you can provide the missing component.

Musician Needs Checklist
   Physical Needs
      ❏ A quiet space—a "practice room"
      ❏ An instrument in good working condition
      ❏ Sheet music, including a method book, developmental books, and solo music

❑ A music stand to place sheet music at the correct eye level
❑ A pencil (Musicians shouldn't use a pen because they often need to erase marks and rewrite sections.)
❑ A metronome, a small device that tracks the beat
❑ A tuner, a device that helps musicians learn when their instrument is in tune
❑ Extra materials, depending on the instrument (These are discussed in appendix C. Check with your music director if you have any questions.)

Psychological Needs
❑ Energy—without mental energy, a musician does not stand a chance
❑ Focus—be sure your child focuses on the things that need to get done, not just the things that are fun to do
❑ A goal—without a clear goal, your child will waste time
❑ Analytical skills—the ability to determine what is wrong and how to fix it
❑ A positive self-image and self-confidence
❑ Support and encouragement in the home and school environment

WHAT YOU CAN DO

When starting a new instrument, children need to know that they will not sound like a professional. Many beginning musicians think that they will sound great from day one. They're wrong. It takes a lot of hard work over a long period of time to sound great. Prepare your musician to work hard and to focus on learning new and challenging skills.

Additionally, help your child to develop good habits in instrument care. By sending a clear message about the importance of caring for and treating a musical instrument with respect, parents also will be telling their children to take care of and have respect for themselves. Always encourage your musician to think long term. Great rewards will eventually follow when children can express themselves in a unique way!

Even if you know little or nothing about music or the instrument that your child is learning, you can make the difference in your child's success. By reinforcing regular practice, providing for your musician's physical and psychological needs, and being a constant source of encouragement, you help boost your child's enthusiasm and determination to succeed in music. Take the Helping Your Child Master Good Practice Habits quiz to learn if you are doing all that you can to help your child practice and be successful.

Helping Your Child Master Good Practice Habits: A Quiz for Parents

- ❏ Have you ensured that your child has an established place to practice?
- ❏ Does your child have an established time to practice?
- ❏ Does your child have a regular routine for practice?
- ❏ Does your musician break apart challenging phrases and master material before moving on?
- ❏ Do you make sure that your child stops to fix mistakes instead of playing through them?
- ❏ Do you encourage your child to practice trouble spots slowly until he or she gets them right?
- ❏ Does your musician mark his or her music with a pencil, dividing it into sections, and then practice the sections that are marked?
- ❏ Do you make sure your child sets a clear goal and writes it down before practicing?
- ❏ Do you monitor and review your child's goals regularly?
- ❏ Do you help your child set school-related goals (such as learning music assigned in band class) and private/individual goals (such as putting on a miniperformance for family and friends in your home)?
- ❏ Does your child practice a minimum of twenty minutes per day, five days a week?
- ❏ Do you review your child's practice sessions regularly and enthusiastically?
- ❏ Did you purchase a fantastic program called Smart Music, which is available at www.smartmusic.com?

MISCONCEPTIONS ABOUT PRACTICE

It is important to understand why many aspiring musicians don't practice regularly. In addition to not knowing what or how to practice, they may have misconceptions about what a good practice session is really like. Take a look at the Practice Realities box and read the misconceptions. Have you heard your child make any of these statements about practice? Now read the reality statements carefully and talk about these issues with your child, exploring why your child might be resistant to practice and how to change his or her attitude toward it.

Practice Realities

Misconception: It's boring.
Reality: It's only as boring as you make it.

Misconception: It's punishment.
Reality: Practice should never be used as punishment.

Misconception: It's repetitive.
Reality: Repetition, when used properly, is one of the key elements to improvement. The more you repeat the right exercises, the more you will improve.

Misconception: You need to practice six hours a day in order to be any good.
Reality: For most musicians, twenty to thirty solid minutes of practice is adequate to gain a moderate level of success.

Misconception: I can do it alone.
Reality: Although you should practice by yourself, you need focus and guidance. If you hope to be first chair or to create music effortlessly, then a private teacher can be very helpful.

Misconception: It can be done anywhere.
Reality: You can practice in many different places; however, a special place like a practice room, complete with a light, a chair, a music stand, and a pencil, is ideal.

Misconception: Practice should be done every day.
Reality: It is good to practice regularly because muscle strength, coordination, and confidence will improve, but a break for a day or two is often necessary to maintain mental and physical health.

THE TOP FIVE EXCUSES

Student musicians have five main excuses for why they don't practice. I will describe each one and then share a brief story about one of my students to illustrate what kind of impact the excuse can have on a musician. Excuses are not good in music. For that matter, they are not good in life! Encourage your child to practice, no matter what, without excuses!

Disorganization and Lack of Time

It's interesting how there is always enough time to do things like watch television, but not enough time to do other things like practice music. In order to become musicians, children must take responsibility for themselves and become dedicated to improving. This means making a commitment. Aspiring musicians must want to improve. Sometimes practicing music gets rough, but with a little preparation and motivation, your child will be able to overcome just about anything. Make success a habit—encourage practice every day! The following story shows how one saxophone player was able to get organized and fit practice into her after-school schedule.

Sarah, a sixth-grade saxophone player in my band, was a bright girl with great musical talent—one of those beginning students who enjoys music and plays naturally. As the school year progressed, Sarah's high grades and expressive musical qualities started to wane. I asked her why her playing was suffering, and she said, "I can't seem to prepare enough for the tests; it always seems like something is going on." Interested in seeing Sarah improve, I asked her approximately how much time elapsed between arriving home from school and going to sleep.

Sarah thought about it and replied, "About seven hours. Why?"

I said, "I'd like you to decide on a thirty-minute block of time each day when you will practice. You have seven hours to choose from."

Sarah said, "There's a show I like to watch, so I'll practice thirty minutes before it every day."

As Sarah started to take responsibility for her actions and her success, she became able to prepare a schedule that helped her improve. As simple as it may seem, it was a very important accomplishment: she got organized! By planning a practice time each night before her favorite program, Sarah used her own interests to motivate herself and take responsibility for her own success.

Vision and Focus

Many beginning musicians understandably suffer from lack of knowledge, understanding, and general get-the-job-done know-how. Since improvement is the goal, what do successful musicians practice, and how exactly do they do it? Sometimes when young musicians sit down to practice, they don't have the vision or focus of more experienced musicians. They can't concentrate on specific goals and don't have a good sense of where they're headed. Natasha's story shows how one musician was able to learn to practice with a clear vision and a sense of purpose.

Natasha was a promising young cellist, bright and energetic with a good attitude. She always tried hard in rehearsals and had a regular practice schedule, working diligently every night for at least half an hour, sometimes more. Yet she didn't seem to be improving as quickly as she should have been.

One day I asked Natasha how her practice sessions were going, and she said that every time she sat down to practice, she would play the hard parts over and over just as I told her to, but for some reason she couldn't quite see what she was working toward.

I said, "Natasha, before you sit down to practice, take a few minutes to think and relax. Imagine yourself as a professional cellist. Imagine you're in the New York Philharmonic playing a big concert. Or that you're Yo-Yo Ma playing a solo in front of thousands of people. Think about how you want to play. Hear the sounds in your head. Hum or sing them aloud. Imagine you're a virtuoso and you have all that knowledge and experience and vision. Then sit down to practice."

Natasha tried the new technique for a week. One day after class she came up to me and said, "I think I'm getting better. I can see where I'm going now. When I imagine I'm a pro, I begin to sound like one!"

Bad Time, Bad Place

Musicians need space to practice, space to experiment, and space to explore. Does your home lack a space where your child is free to practice?

Musicians who do not have a quiet, well-lit place to practice are at a serious disadvantage and will be unable to grow. A young musician named Matthew was able to practice despite not having a suitable place for studying music at home.

Matthew, a bright alto saxophone player, was from a single-parent home and lived in a small two-bedroom apartment. Upon getting his instrument and joining the band, he won his seating challenges and moved into a first-chair position.

After several months, Matthew's seating rank began to drop. I noticed his waning enthusiasm but couldn't understand his failure to improve. He seemed to enjoy playing music. His toes would tap to the beat, and his eyes would brighten as he played. His lack of progress remained a mystery.

After class I talked to Matthew. He shared with me that though he had an unwavering commitment to music, he wasn't able to practice at home anymore. There had been complaints about the noise from the neighbors in the next apartment—so many that he could not practice.

Later that night, I called Matthew's mother and discussed the issue with her. She agreed to allow Matthew to practice after school in my band room. In no time, his playing and his self-esteem improved.

Family Expectations—or Lack Thereof

A family that does not make practice and improvement a priority will greatly reduce the chances of success. As a parent, how can you create an environment that encourages musical excellence? To begin with, purchase a good-quality instrument and related materials, establish a regular practice space and time, and listen to your child play and provide positive comments for support. Every child progresses at a different rate, but after working with thousands of families, I have noticed one big difference between musicians who move ahead and those who lag behind: families that create a nurturing environment with high expectations of musical excellence tend to produce better musicians at a faster rate. One mom was determined for her son to get ahead—and he did.

The moment I first saw Joy, mother of my newest clarinet player Ryan, soon to be known as "first-chair Ry," I knew she was an outstanding parent. I arrived at my music room on a crisp September morning at the beginning of the school year to find Joy eagerly waiting with Ryan, who had instrument in hand and was ready to play.

Joy said, "I'd like to introduce myself and my son Ryan. We want to encourage Ryan to be a success in music. What do we need to do in order for him to become a good musician?"

I don't usually meet parents who are so focused and proactive about their child's musical success. I knew instantly that Ryan was going to start off on exactly the right foot, and it would be only a matter of time before he became a great musician. Is it surprising that after only one year of learning the clarinet, first-chair Ry jumped up to advanced band? Strong nurturing and parental support fueled his advancement.

The Easy Way Out

Most people enjoy working on things they are already proficient at, and for musicians this can be dangerous. It's important to learn and master new material. For musicians who continually play familiar music that they can already play well, a new piece of music can be frustrating. Consequently, musicians who don't push themselves to learn new music end up short-changing themselves. Persistence, determination, and goal setting can help overcome this problem. Briana's story illustrates how one violinist was able to overcome her fear of learning new material.

Briana played the violin in intermediate orchestra. Her playing was proficient, but because she preferred to play the same songs over and over, she had a limited solo repertoire. In a nutshell, she was the type of musician who was easily frustrated with new pieces and refused to learn them. In the fall, when all-city honor orchestra audition dates were posted, Briana seemed interested, and I thought that perhaps I could turn this into a positive learning experience.

The day audition announcements were made, Briana was perturbed. She could not figure out why musicians had to play unfamiliar music. I explained to her that what makes an honor orchestra "an honor" is the fact that all the outstanding musicians are able to learn new and challenging literature.

I asked her to use active-practice techniques on her new solo music. Briana found that the solo, though seemingly difficult, was organized into distinct sections, much like her old solos. After a week of practicing, she could play the entire piece well—both the easy and the hard parts! Four weeks later, she made it into the first violin section of the all-city orchestra.

THE END OF BAD PRACTICE HABITS

The following section, "Mastering Motivation," will allow you to help your child combat the top excuses that most musicians face. The ideas are categorized into three sections—basic, intermediate, and advanced levels—and are written for your musician. Share these ideas with your child, talking about what excuses stand in his or her way, and ask your child to try some of the suggested activities to overcome them. You may want to copy these pages for your musician to refer to whenever he or she needs an idea.

Mastering Motivation

> *Excuse: Lack of Organization*
> *Basic*
>
> - Tackle something new that you would not normally undertake.
> - Learn two new pieces of music, one slow and one fast.
>
> *Intermediate*
>
> - Ask a better musician for help on a piece of music.
> - Help someone else on a piece of music.
> - Organize a miniconcert or chamber concert where you and your friends perform and listen to each other play. Rate your performances (and afterward, celebrate your hard work together).
>
> *Advanced*
>
> - Compose a piece of music to perform before the next meal or special event.
> - Compose a minipiece entirely in your head and perform it.

- Write an essay on how music relates to other areas of your life and how it makes you feel.

Your Ideas

- _____
- _____

Excuse: Lack of Vision and Focus
Basic

- Play a piece from the beginning of your method book. Learn about the history and culture surrounding its composition.
- Listen to a recorded piece of music and describe events as they happen. (For example, a violin enters followed by a drum.)
- At a professional concert, read the concert notes in the program and then listen to the concert while keeping the information from the notes in mind. See if you can identify significant musical events.

Intermediate

- Play two completely different styles of music (for example, slow and fast, or high and low).
- Play a solo with a piano accompaniment.
- Play some varied styles of music in a small chamber group, like a trio or quartet.

Advanced

- Write an essay on how music relates to other areas of your life and how it makes you feel.
- Improvise a basic song with a live or computerized recording of chords.
- Compose a short piece of music that mimics an emotion.

Your Ideas

- _____
- _____

Excuse: Bad Environment
Basic

- Practice in a well-lit, quiet room with a chair, a music stand, and a pencil.
- Practice with the television, radio, computer, and telephone off—or better yet, in a room without these distractions.

Intermediate

- Practice in a new and different place—one that inspires you.
- Practice with your best friend.
- If you normally practice alone, practice with your parent in the room. If you normally practice with someone in the room, practice alone.
- Practice early in the morning instead of late at night.

Advanced

- Practice on a concert stage with the lights on.
- Try playing on a different instrument, such as a professional-quality instrument.
- Practice twice as long as you normally do.
- Listen to your solo with a professional playing your part. Write down all the ways you can play like him or her and then do it!
- Practice music after listening to your pieces.

Your Ideas

- _____
- _____

Excuse: Support and Lifestyle
Basic

- Make music a priority in your life.
- Practice regularly.

- Celebrate success.
- Listen to live concert performances.

Intermediate

- Perform for others.
- Join a band or orchestra at school.
- Learn a second instrument.

Advanced

- Work hard and play hard.
- Work with a private teacher.
- Join a summer music camp.
- Invite parents and family to your special concerts.

Your Ideas

- _____
- _____

Excuse: Lack of Determination
Basic

- During your practice session, write down your achievements.
- Listen to a music concert from a group that is at or near the same level as your group.
- Develop a routine.

Intermediate

- Find a small section of music that seems difficult or impossible to play and master it in thirty minutes or less.
- Play occasionally with a friend who inspires you.
- Create a simple song that might be used on your favorite television show.
- Listen to a recording of a professional group and write down what you hear.
- Play a small section of music from memory.

Advanced

- Concentrate for ten minutes on playing a passage while mastering only *one* of the following characteristics: rhythm, tone, or expression.
- Memorize an entire solo.
- Break your practice session down into small, manageable parts.
- Take an easy piece of music and play it up or down an octave.

Your Ideas

- _____
- _____

WHAT PARENTS WANT TO KNOW ABOUT PRACTICING

What should my child practice every day?

Help your child stay focused on his or her goals, but keep in mind that all work and no play is not much fun—and if music is not fun, at least on some level, most children will not want to practice it! Make sure your child mixes challenging sections with fun pieces for a healthy balance.

What should I do while my child is practicing?

Encourage your child to perform for you at the end of the practice session, sharing areas of success and pieces that still need work. You should compliment your child often. It is also important to encourage your child to review areas that are still rough. Ask your child questions about what is fun to play, and encourage him or her to learn new songs.

My child just wants to have fun. What can I say to make practice more appealing?

Learning how to play an instrument can be frustrating. While siblings watch TV and friends talk on the telephone or play ball outside, it may not seem fair to be inside practicing. In all honesty, practicing is hard work. If your child sees only the hard work, practicing can turn into a terrible chore. Seeing the rewards of music is not easy if your child is trying to do it alone. A family can positively impact the progress and development of a musician by encouraging regular miniconcerts and performances. Centering musical development and performance on important family activities like dinner and family reunions quickly teaches children the power and influence of music.

What do I tell my child who just doesn't want to practice, or worse yet, wants to quit music altogether?

First, ascertain if your child is truly unhappy and wants to quit or is just having a bad day. Recognize that nearly all musicians will come to a point where quitting will seem easier than continuing. Encouraging words are helpful and motivating. Most musicians who want to quit tend to fall under one or more of the following categories: they are disorganized; they don't understand how to gain access to musical knowledge and skills; their musical environment is not challenging or fulfilling, or it doesn't encourage sustained musical excellence; or they simply do not have the determination to succeed. If your child falls into one of these categories, review the activities in the "Mastering Motivation" section. Also keep in mind that some people love music but are more attracted to other arts and disciplines, and they should be encouraged to pursue excellence in those areas when appropriate.

TAKING THE NEXT STEP

Once your child begins to develop good practice habits, you will start to see and hear a difference. Can you detect behavioral improvements that will likely affect other parts of your musician's life? Can you hear the musical improvements? The improvements might include any of the following:

- Improved sound—range, tone, flexibility
- Improved problem-solving skills
- Ability to set priorities
- Result-oriented behavior
- Improved time-management skills
- Improved focus
- Creativity
- Flexibility

- Emotional and intellectual engagement
- Satisfaction

Now what do you do to make your child improve even more? Try some of the following suggestions, or refer to the "Mastering Motivation" section for more ideas.

- Ask your child to perform a miniconcert every week at a special time, such as Saturday night after dinner.
- Engage your child in discussions about music. Even if you don't have a musical background, you can talk about how music relates to other areas of your life and how it makes you feel.
- Listen to recorded music with your child and ask him or her to describe what instruments are playing and other elements of the performance. Encourage your child to use musical terms (e.g., melody, rhythm, staccato, legato) and to define them for you.
- Ask your child to memorize a piece of music and perform it for you from memory.
- Encourage your child to compose a piece of music and perform it at a special family event.

• 5 •

Practice Smart:
Strategies for Young Musicians

Challenge is a dragon with a gift in its mouth. . . .
Tame the dragon and the gift is yours.

—Noela Evans

JUST FOR YOU . . . THE MUSICIAN

Many young musicians and their parents understand how important consistency and dedication are to achieving musical success, yet they commonly find that they do not understand exactly what they should be doing during a practice session. Written for the young musician, this chapter focuses on improving musical abilities, developing time-management skills, and setting realistic but challenging goals for a practice session. It provides a number of tools—challenge sheets, checklists, and a quiz—that can be photocopied and used multiple times in guiding a musician through practice sessions. Parents may want to read this chapter with their children or encourage them to read it on their own.

First, I'm going to tell you my story about how I learned to practice efficiently, and then I'm going to share practice strategies that I've developed in my years as a musician and band director. Remember, you don't have to use everything in this chapter all at once. In fact, by applying just a couple of the ideas to each practice session, you'll find that you become more focused and successful.

AN ALL-AMERICAN STORY

When I was a sixteen-year-old junior in high school, I was presented with an enormous and nearly impossible challenge: to audition against thousands of other musicians from every state in the union for 1 seat of 102 in the highly competitive McDonald's All-American Band. The judges accepted only two people per state and two from the District of Columbia.

I am from California, which has a population of 34 million. I knew that I had more competition than musicians coming from states like Connecticut (population 3.5 million) and Rhode Island (population 1.1 million).

I received a huge amount of difficult (and almost impossible) music in the mail. I had about two weeks to learn and master all of it, record it, and send in the recording for review. I organized the music by level of difficulty. Bit by bit, I learned each and every note. I spent hours refining and perfecting each part so that I would play perfectly.

In the end, this great challenge didn't deter me; it inspired me. After carefully reviewing the music and meticulously practicing all the parts, I eventually won a position in the All-American Band. And later, I even became the All-American representative for the entire band.

I want to share with you a few important things that I learned from this experience:

- Always play your best.
- Time is limited, so isolate and practice the things that need work.
- Break down music into small, manageable parts and learn them bit by bit.
- Think about your playing and respond to the music emotionally and intellectually.
- Express yourself through your instrument; make a statement.

CHALLENGE SHEETS

No matter how you ultimately decide to organize your practice sessions, you'll need to track your work. This is why I have created challenge sheets

Table 5.1. Challenge Sheet

Day	Challenge/Task	Success +/–	Time	Signature
Monday				
Tuesday				
Wednesday				
Thursday				
Friday				
Saturday				
Sunday				

(table 5.1), forms that help you organize and document your goals and progress. You chart your progress by writing down specific goals and addressing main issues in your practice. You should have a pile of these sheets on hand so that you can fill them out for each practice session. They take only a few minutes a day, and they work!

For each practice session, follow the instructions below to fill out your challenge sheet.

1. Locate the day of the week in the left column.
2. Now you will need to think of specific goals to write in the "Challenge/Task" column. Ask your music teacher and parents to help you think of goals. Write down exactly what you're going to play. After you've had some practice filling out challenge sheets, it will be easier to think of goals, and you may not need to ask for help each time. Be sure to fill in only one day's goals at a time, because your goals may change from day to day as you reevaluate your progress.
3. Practice, focusing on your goals for the day.
4. Now play a miniconcert for your parents, showing them what you learned that day. You should also play the parts you're still having trouble with, so that when you learn them they'll see how much progress you've made.
5. When you're finished playing, evaluate your goals again and decide whether you met them or not. In the "Success" column, give

yourself a plus for each goal you've met and a minus for goals that still need work. Be sure to review your scores with your parents. If you have all pluses or all minuses, you need to reevaluate your goals and see if they're too easy or too hard. For every ten marks, you should have a ratio of about eight pluses and two minuses. By the end of a week, you'll be able to see if you're making consistent progress toward your goals. You might also find it helpful to write brief comments in the "Success" column about what you still need to work on.

6. In the "Time" column, write down how many minutes you practiced.

7. Now ask your parents to review your challenge sheet entries for the day. Talk to them about your goals for your next practice session and any worries you might have. Talk about your successes and failures. Then ask your parents to write any comments they might have and sign in the "Signature" column. Now your challenge sheet for the day is complete!

Filling out your challenge sheets will get easier over time. It's a good idea to keep them all together in a binder, so that you can review your progress over the long term and celebrate your success. See Alex's challenge sheet (table 5.2) for an example of what a completed sheet might look like. Note that Alex's goals include school-related projects and personal challenges like performing at home and church.

STOP PLAYING STRAIGHT THROUGH!

Have you ever played a difficult piece of music over and over and just couldn't quite get it right? Did you find that some parts—with long, slow notes—were easy and you played them well, while other parts—with short, fast notes and difficult fingerings—were hard and you ended up stumbling over them every time, no matter how many times you played the piece? I've developed a solution to this problem: active practice.

The first thing you need to do is stop playing your music all the way through—right away. It's a big waste of time when you're still learning a piece. If you take the piece apart and concentrate on the hard sections,

Table 5.2. Alex's Challenge Sheet

Day	Challenge/Task	Success +/−	Time	Signature
Monday	Play lines 27–33 in schoolbook; work out notes, fingerings, and rhythms; begin solo work	+	30	Perfect Parent
Tuesday	Review new notes on lines 27–28 Work on first half of solo on page 33	+ − (Still need to work on solo)	30	Perfect Parent
Wednesday	Continue work on first half of solo on page 33	+	45	Perfect Parent
Thursday	Work on in-class music Memorize warm-up from line 29	+ +	30	Perfect Parent
Friday	Memorize scale from line 31 Work on second half of solo on page 33 Perform solo for family	− (Still need to work on scale) + +	 60	Perfect Parent Perfect Parent
Saturday	Rest day			
Sunday	Play at church service	+	75	Perfect Parent

when you put it all back together, you'll be able to perform it perfectly, from beginning to end. To get started, work through the three methods I outline below. You can practice the musical examples printed here, or you can apply these techniques to your own music.

Method One: Break Apart Difficult Sections

Step One   Look through your music and isolate the difficult sections. With a pencil, circle or bracket all the hard parts. That way, you can focus on learning them, rather than skipping over them or struggling through them. Difficult sections might have fast notes, unusually high or low notes, large jumps or skips, complicated key signatures and transitions, lots of accidentals, or something uniquely challenging (for example, an unusual rhythm). See figure 5.1 for examples.

Flute

Practice fast notes in measure 3.

Tuba

0   12 0   12 1   0 12   0   1   0 12   1

Practice fast notes in measures 5 and 6 and write down fingerings.

Clarinet in Bb

Practice fast and challenging
notes in measures 4 and 5.

Figure 5.1.   Musical Challenges

Step Two   Practice each section you marked in step one until you get it right. Don't move on until you can play it correctly. Follow these steps:

1. Write in difficult fingerings and note names.
2. Practice each marked section slowly.
3. Sing, whistle, hum, or imagine hearing the music in your head before playing. Pretend that you're a professional and you can do anything . . . how would you play it?
4. Use a metronome to help you track and improve time and rhythm.
5. Repeat. The key to learning (and mastering) a section of music is to learn it slowly and then repeat, repeat, repeat. The correct number of repetitions is the number of times you need to master the part . . . don't be surprised if it takes many tens or hundreds of times! Don't move on to method two until you've learned all the tough sections.

Method Two: Put It Back Together

Step One Go back to a few measures before the difficult passage that you just learned. Now start here and see if you can play through the difficult section without stopping and making mistakes. Make sure you can play your music perfectly. If you're still having trouble, go back and review the hard passage. Don't forget: repetition is the key!

Step Two Add on a few measures after the difficult section that you just learned. Now see if you can play a few measures before the difficult section, through the difficult section, and a few measures after the difficult section without making any mistakes. If you stumble on a few notes or must stop, review the hard passage yet again. When you repeat it correctly, enjoy your success! Now keep adding more measures until you can play the whole piece!

Look at the example in figure 5.2 to see how you can take a challenging piece apart and then put it back together.

Method Three: Tackle the Hardest, Longest Parts

This method is good for very difficult and long sections. For example, say you just circled four large sections of a difficult piece of music. What should you do next? How can you possibly learn this huge amount of music?

1. Use Method One to learn the challenging parts in measures 6 and 8.

2. Start at measure 4 and play through the difficult passage to the beginning of measure 9.

3. Add two or more measures after the challenging passage. Play measures 6 through 12, then try playing measures 4 through 12.

Figure 5.2.   A Cellist Practices Mozart's Divertimenti

1. Measures 5, 6, 7, 10, 11, 12, and 13 are challenging because of the speed and range of the notes.

2. Break the challenging sections down further and learn them piece by piece.

3. If you are having trouble putting the pieces back together, learn measures one at a time. For example, isolate measure 11 and work on it.

Figure 5.3.   A Violinist Practices Mozart's Divertimenti

Step One   Circle or bracket the difficult passage.

Step Two   Within the passage, break down the phrase further into small, learnable minisections. Then apply the strategies from method one to learn these smaller bits. As you learn the notes one by one, you can slowly put the sections back together by adding notes and measures. But remember, don't move on until you know each note perfectly! For an example of how this works, see figure 5.3.

As you can see, there is a lot to do for effective practicing. A straight run-through of your music just won't get the job done. Repeat these three methods as often as necessary on each new piece of music, and in no time you'll be playing the easy and the hard parts with confidence and skill.

THREE PRACTICE SESSIONS THAT WORK

How long should you practice? What exactly should you do during a practice session? I've developed three practice sessions based on units of time that you should find easy to follow: the Thirty-Minute Session, the Sixty-to-Ninety-Minute Session, and the Marathon Session. You don't have to practice for exactly the amount of time named in each session. Instead of watching the clock, focus on achieving specific goals from your challenge sheets. At the end of each session, ask yourself, "Did I learn what I needed to learn?" If you did, then ultimately the quantity of time you spent doing the activity is *quality* time.

Pre-practice

The sessions begin with a pre-practice time when you prepare physically and mentally. You set up your special practice place, turn lights on, and turn the television off. You also set your goals for this particular practice session and write them down on a challenge sheet. This period lasts from less than a minute up to ten minutes, depending on which session you're doing.

Warm-up

The warm-up time is next. For most musicians, this section will be nearly identical from day to day. You should choose warm-up exercises that improve consistency, accuracy, tone development, counting, and strength. Ask your teacher or parents if you need help selecting an appropriate warm-up. A good warm-up, played over time, will help improve your self-confidence and technical accuracy. This period lasts between four and twenty minutes.

Review

A good way to ease into your practice session is to review key concepts from your school rehearsal that day or from an earlier practice. Frequent repetition of recently learned material will reinforce your knowledge and help you master new concepts. This period lasts from five to thirty-five minutes.

Learn New Material

In most cases, the bulk of your practice time will be spent on learning new music. Be sure to stay focused, and remember that learning new material can be very challenging. This period lasts between ten minutes and an hour.

Play Something Fun

This is *your* fun time. Show off and perform for others. Play what you really enjoy the most, even if it's easy or silly. It's important to allow for fun time and reward yourself for all of your hard work. This time lasts between five and fifteen minutes.

Cool-Down

Only the Sixty-to-Ninety-Minute and Marathon practice sessions have this period, which lasts between five and fifteen minutes. This time gives you a chance to relax muscles that you've been working and review fingerings.

Postpractice

During this important time, you should reflect on what went well and what didn't during your session. Finish filling out your challenge sheet, and talk to your parents about your progress. This period takes between one and five minutes.

The time line in figure 5.4 shows the progression of the practice session.

WHICH PRACTICE SESSION SHOULD YOU USE?

You don't have to pick just one type of practice session and stick with it. In fact, it's healthy to mix things up a little and take on different challenges. For example, you might use the Thirty-Minute Session on most days, but once a week challenge yourself with the Sixty-to-Ninety-Minute Session. Or if you're preparing for a big concert, you might even try the Marathon Session. Tables 5.3, 5.4, and 5.5 break down the sessions into sections, listing the amount of time you should spend on each part of the practice.

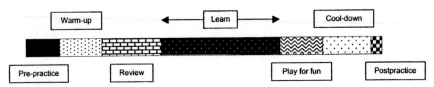

Figure 5.4.   Practice Time Line

As a general rule of thumb, the Thirty-Minute Session is designed for the younger musician in elementary or middle school, or for the older musician who has limited time and energy to practice. The Sixty-to-Ninety-Minute Session can be used by any musician in elementary, middle, or high school. The Marathon Session is designed for the experienced musician in middle school, high school, or college and beyond. Although a good physical and mental challenge, the Marathon Session should not be overused. As the saying goes, practice makes perfect, but too much practice could actually be detrimental to long-term development. You don't ever want to start feeling burned out or that music is a terrible chore. Use the Practice Session Checklist to evaluate how you're doing in your sessions.

Table 5.3.   Thirty-Minute Practice Session

Section	Time (min.)	Helpful Hints
Pre-practice	0	You need a quiet, well-lit room with a chair, a music stand, and a pencil.
Warm-up	4	There are many written warm-ups available. Play one that incorporates long tones, slurs, and range, then play one that moves through the major and minor keys.
Review Recently Learned Concept/Material	5–10	There are unique concepts presented in rehearsal or private lessons such as how to produce a sound, count, and perform. Review these concepts and master them.
Learn New Material	10	This is often the hardest section to do well. It takes unique skills and focus to learn something new or improve on a skill.
Play Something Fun for Yourself	5	Have fun! Most musicians already do this very well.
Postpractice	1	Take a moment to review and celebrate your success while simultaneously noting areas that need further attention and work. Have a parent or family member comment on your progress. Chart your work on a challenge sheet.

Total time: 30 minutes

Table 5.4. Sixty-to-Ninety-Minute Practice Session

Section	Time (min.)	Helpful Hints
Pre-practice	0	You need a quiet, well-lit room with a chair, a music stand, and a pencil.
Warm-up	5–15	There are many written warm-ups available. Play one that incorporates long tones, slurs, and range, then play one that moves through the major and minor keys.
Review Recently Learned Concept/Material	15–25	There are unique concepts presented in rehearsal or private lessons such as how to produce a sound, count, and perform. Review these concepts and master them.
Learn New Material	20–30	This is often the hardest section to do well. It takes unique skills and focus to learn something new or improve on a skill.
Play Something Fun for Yourself	10	Have fun! Most musicians already do this very well.
Cool-Down	5–10	This segment will assist in relaxing muscles while reviewing important fingering patterns. Think of it as preparation for your next practice session.
Postpractice	5	Take a moment to review and celebrate your success while simultaneously noting areas that need further attention and work. Have a parent or family member comment on your progress. Chart your work on a challenge sheet.

Total time: 60–90 minutes

Table 5.5. Marathon Practice Session

Section	Time (min.)	Helpful Hints
Pre-practice	5–10	You need a quiet, well-lit room with a chair, a music stand, and a pencil. You will soon use specific muscles for an extended period of time, so stretch appropriately—hands, arm, neck, back, diaphragm, and legs. Spend several minutes doing preparatory breathing exercises.
Warm-up	10–20	There are many written warm-ups available. Play one that incorporates long tones, slurs, and range, then play one that moves through the major and minor keys. Also play one that moves through all the major/minor keys in a slow and controlled manner.
Review Recently Learned Concept/Material	25–35	There are unique concepts presented in rehearsals or private lessons such as how to produce a sound, count, and perform. Review these concepts and master them.
Learn New Material	30–60	This is often the hardest section to do well. It takes unique skills and focus to learn something new or improve on a skill.
Play Something Fun for Yourself	15	Have fun! Most musicians already do this very well.
Cool-Down	10–15	This segment will assist in relaxing muscles while reviewing important fingering patterns. Think of it as preparation for your next practice session.
Postpractice	5	Take a moment to review and celebrate your success while simultaneously noting areas that need further attention and work. Have a parent or family member comment on your progress. Chart your work on a challenge sheet.

Total time: 100–160 minutes

PRACTICE SESSION CHECKLIST

Do you . . .

- [ ] have a quiet, well-lit room with a chair, a music stand, music, and a pencil?
- [ ] have an established warm-up to play?
- [ ] review music or a concept that you recently learned?
- [ ] isolate (either circle or highlight) a new section of music that you need to learn?
- [ ] review the music that you just learned by playing it over and over many times?
- [ ] play something that you enjoy just for the fun of it?
- [ ] take a moment to play for someone and demonstrate your newly acquired skills or finely tuned musicianship?
- [ ] carefully organize your practice time?
- [ ] complete every step of your practice session?
- [ ] accomplish your goals?
- [ ] track your sessions on a challenge sheet?

70/30: ANOTHER KIND OF PRACTICE SESSION

Have you ever started an activity like a hobby, a sport, or music feeling excited, only to hit a wall, sputter out, and feel like quitting? Occasionally I see this happen to musicians. Or do you ever feel that even though you're playing all the right notes, there's something missing from your performance? I often see musicians who only play the notes. The internal energy and meaning within the notes, the silence after the notes, the beautiful arching of the phrases—all of these things are somehow missing. The end result is that little music is actually mastered. A big problem indeed!

To overcome these serious and frustrating burn-out types of problems, I developed a simple technique that will help focus learning and develop musical mastery. I call this technique the 70/30 Practice Rule, and I am confident that it will help you understand music and become a better musician.

The 70/30 Practice Rule works like this: While learning new material, spend 70 percent of your time and energy concentrating on new, unlearned, and not-yet-mastered parts. This includes figuring out rhythms; learning notes, fingerings, and positions; writing in note names; figuring out appropriate playing techniques; marking off phrases; and finding patterns. Then spend 30 percent of your time and energy reviewing and evaluating what you just learned. Play things slowly and repeatedly, reinforcing the correct actions and movements. In the long run, reviewing material results in significant improvement and refined musicianship.

The 70/30 Practice Rule is a practice session itself. On the days you use it, you won't need to use the Thirty-Minute, Sixty-to-Ninety-Minute, or Marathon practice sessions. The 70/30 session should be used as an inspiring change of pace from your regular practice sessions. If you find your regular sessions becoming tedious or boring, you may want to spice things up by sight-reading a new piece using the 70/30 Practice Rule. The following first-person account tells how a chamber orchestra violinist named Jason used the 70/30 Practice Rule to get out of a rut.

A Change of Pace

I noticed my practice routine started to become boring, and I found myself feeling like I'd rather watch television or call my friends than practice. These feelings started to increase, and at one point I even thought, "Why should I play music at all?"

One day after rehearsal, my band director noticed my low energy level. He recommended that I try practicing a new solo. He suggested that I spend 70 percent of my time on the hardest parts (circle the hardest parts, then practice them like crazy) and spend 30 percent of my time reviewing everything else. At the end of my practice session, I would play the solo for my parents—and the following day at rehearsal for the entire class.

I did it, and it worked! I practically forgot about my normal routine because I had a goal and a way to achieve it. I worked very hard to be a success. I was totally immersed and motivated.

Moving Forward by Stepping Backward

You might be thinking, "Why would I want to play the same things over and over for 70 percent of my practice time?" It's a good question. If you want to keep getting better and better and learning new music, then it might seem counterproductive to work on the same things over and over. After all, why would you want to spend *more* time reviewing something that is difficult? The first time you review the material, it might feel as though you're taking two steps backward.

But review is an essential element of practice that all good musicians must come to understand. Review leads to the mastery of material. Taking two steps backward initially can eventually move you three or even four steps forward. This is why review is so important. It propels musicians forward.

The 70/30 Practice Rule is designed to help you concentrate most of your time and energy on reviewing the parts that really need work. Use the 70/30 Practice Rule Checklist to guide you through this motivating type of practice session.

70/30 Practice Rule Checklist

During 70 percent of the time, you should do the following:

- ❑ Identify the new material that you will be working with.
- ❑ Start with the title and composer. See if they affect or inspire the way you interpret the piece. Write down your observations. For example, if you saw that the composer was John Philip Sousa, aka the "March King," you might expect 2/4 time.
- ❑ Write down the key of the piece (look at the key signature) and any times that the key changes throughout the piece.
- ❑ Look up any unfamiliar foreign words that may be written in your music and write down the translations.
- ❑ Identify repeats. Write in arrows or circles marking the repeated sections. If appropriate, mark off all endings clearly.
- ❑ Circle and figure out all unique and difficult rhythms.
- ❑ Circle and figure out all unknown notes. Write in the fingerings.
- ❑ Clearly mark off important phrases, sections, and breathing spots.
- ❑ Work on mastering the new material.

During 30 percent of the time, you should do the following:

❑ Evaluate what you just wrote down. Was it done correctly? Fix mistakes.
❑ Make sure that you wrote down all your fingerings, rhythms, and other important information.
❑ Slowly play through the material that you just learned.
❑ Repeat as many times as necessary in order to play the part fluently.
❑ Eventually speed up your music to at or near the speed at which it ideally should be performed.
❑ Repeat as many times as necessary so that you feel very comfortable with the new music.
❑ Review your challenge sheet.

REVIEW: GOOD PRACTICE HABITS QUIZ

No matter what kind of practice session you use, you can take this quiz to find out if you're practicing effectively. Simply read each question and write a score in the blank: 3 for usually, 2 for sometimes, and 1 for seldom. When you're done, tally up your points. Find out how you did in the key at the bottom of the quiz.

Do you . . .

• practice in a well-lit, quiet place? ___ points
• have a regular time to practice (for example, every day after school)? ___ points
• decide which practice session you are going to use before you start practicing (for example, Thirty-Minute, Sixty-to-Ninety-Minute, Marathon, or 70/30)? ___ points
• set goals for yourself *before* you begin to practice and write them on a challenge sheet? ___ points
• review your progress toward your goals regularly? ___ points
• stop and break apart difficult musical sections? ___ points
• use a pencil when you practice to circle challenging sections and write in fingerings? ___ points

- practice with a metronome or tuner? ___ points
- have school-related goals as well as fun, personal goals? For example, after you learn your school music, do you have fun solos that you learn for yourself? ___ points
- challenge and push yourself to learn new and exciting music and solos? ___ points
- play regular miniconcerts for your parents, family, and friends? ___ points
- take responsibility for your success and never give up? ___ points

Total points: ___

Key

A score of 30 or higher means that you thoroughly understand good practice techniques and are practicing efficiently. A score between 20 and 29 indicates that you may have some practicing deficiencies but are probably on the right track. If you scored below 20, you should consider reviewing this chapter again to find out how you can improve your practice sessions. Remember, learning how to practice smart takes time and effort!

WHAT CHILDREN WANT TO KNOW ABOUT PRACTICING

What is the ideal length of time to practice?

It is impossible to prescribe an ideal amount of practice time for everyone. The bottom line is that the ideal practice time is the amount of time you need in order to be successful. Some people may require thirty minutes of practice while others may require three hours! For the average beginning musician, twenty to thirty minutes, five days a week, should be satisfactory. It's important to have rest days so that you don't burn out.

I've had this instrument for over a week, but I don't sound good when I practice. Why?

Even for the most experienced and seasoned professional, good music takes time to create. Concentrate on developing solid fundamental musical skills, and you will eventually produce a clear, enjoyable sound. Finding success in music will ultimately require you to think long term—not days or weeks, but months and even years. Work hard and have patience.

Sometimes I forget how my new instrument works. I'm not sure I'm holding it properly, and sometimes I can't find the correct notes. What do I do?

Your parents or teacher should supply you with a method book. This book will clearly describe how to hold and play your new instrument. Review this information with your parents. Ask them to look at the way you hold and play your instrument and compare it to the descriptions or diagrams in your book. If you're still having trouble, write down your problem spots, and be sure to ask your teacher about them the next time you're in class.

A lot of the other kids seems more talented than I am. Should I practice more?

People have different natural abilities, and they grow and learn at different rates. If you are making a genuine effort to improve your musical skills and are following the practice techniques outlined in this chapter, then you will eventually succeed. It takes longer for some people than for others to reach a level of music mastery. Remember, sometimes plain old hard work and dedication will take over where raw talent alone might run out.

Some days I just don't feel like practicing. What should I do?

There is a simple solution to this all-too-common practice problem. Just do it. Practice. Don't get caught up in the details. Don't think about how much you don't feel like doing it. Just get out your instrument and get to work. In no time you'll be so caught up in working and improving that you'll forget that you didn't want to practice in the first place!

On other days my practice time seems to whiz by. I look at the clock, and suddenly thirty minutes or even an hour has gone, but it feels like five minutes. What's going on?

You're entering the musical "zone." Have you ever watched a movie that was so good you didn't realize how the time flew by? Have you ever found yourself completely focused on a project, only to find an entire day has passed? If you have, then you know what it's like to enter the "zone." And the musical "zone" is no different. It can happen any time when you are completely focused on the task at hand. A great musical performance can also make you feel as though you're in the "zone." Hard work, focused energy, counting, rhythm, tone, looking, listening, adjusting, compensating . . . once everything clicks into place and you are really into the moment, BANG, the entire show is done and an hour has passed! This happens every day in every town across America, and it's a normal part of doing a good job on something that you care about.

Read the following pointers with your parents and talk them over. If there is anything your parents don't understand, demonstrate it or explain it to them. Young musicians whose parents are actively involved in their musical development often achieve success sooner, so be sure that your parents are involved in your musical adventure!

CHILDREN (AND PARENTS): GO THE EXTRA MILE

- Figure out what style a piece of music should be played in, and try to play it in that style (for example, march style). Prepare it as a solo, and perform it for your family before a meal.
- Challenge yourself to play a piece of music in different styles and at different speeds. After performing the different variations for your parents, talk to them about which version you like best and why. Ask them their opinions too.
- Sing a piece of music as you think a professional might perform it.
- Studies have shown that instrumentalists who vocalize their music tend to learn it better.
- Attend a live concert with your parents. Afterward, discuss what you liked and what you disliked. Talk about what role your instrument had in the concert. Use the musical terms you learned in music class, and define them for your parents.
- Organize a concert with your musical friends, and invite their parents to attend too. You can have a duet, a trio, a quartet, a quintet—the possibilities are endless!
- Enroll in private lessons with the best teacher in your area.

III

SECRETS OF THE PROS

· 6 ·

Building Basics

The more I want to get something done, the less I call it work.

—Richard Bach

THERE HAS TO BE A BETTER WAY!

*Y*our child proudly plays with the door wide open so that the entire world can enjoy and appreciate his or her wonderful sound. You walk over, share an encouraging smile, and quietly shut the door. After about thirty minutes, just as your nerves settle, your musician comes in and says, "Listen to this . . ." and proceeds to HONK and SQUACK.

You think to yourself, "Will this ever end?" Without any warning, your musician looks up at you, smiles, and puts you on the spot with a simple question: "What do you think?"

Uh-oh. You may not know much about music, but your ears clearly tell you that something did *not* sound right. You've been through this before and you think to yourself, "Do I tell the truth this time—that it sounded terrible—or do I say something else that will get me out of here?" You bob your head up and down and say, "Nice job! Keep working on it."

You may have had little or no formal music training, but your child still needs support and constructive advice. A key point I never forget when listening to musicians who are just starting out is that everyone wants to improve and sound good—everyone!

But most parents provide little more than a head nod and a supportive "sounds good." Surely there are better ways to help, aren't there? Keep reading and you will find out exactly how to listen, respond, and inspire!

The concepts in this section are presented as your musician will most likely encounter and learn them in a school or private lesson setting. Once you are familiar with them, you can apply them appropriately to inspire your child to focus on something he or she may not even be aware of that needs more work. These "building basics" consist of the primary focal themes for beginning musicians. They are tone, intonation, tempo, and rhythm. The next chapter, "Focus on Musicality," will be great for parents and teachers who want to make a tremendous impact on their child's advanced musical development.

MY TURNING POINT

I'm not exactly sure how my father learned how to talk with me about music, but I'll never forget the wonderful day when, after listening to a solo (which I didn't play very well), my father said to me, "You did a good job. But keep working on it. Focus a bit more on your tone and rhythm." My jaw hit the floor! It felt like we were finally speaking the same musical language. This is the precise moment when I really became motivated and began to strive toward excellence and yearn for advanced musicality.

YOUR CHALLENGE

Simple examples are listed below each term for fast and easy understanding. Learning these terms will be easy, and employing them at just the right moment will be very effective. You'll inspire your child to be the most creative and expressive musician he or she can be!

TONE

Tone refers to the quality or characteristic sound that your child produces while playing. In music, the terms *sound* and *tone* are used interchangeably. They mean the same thing. What do you hear when your child plays? A warm, beautiful, and enticing sound or a crass, shrill noise? When you comment to your child about "playing with good tone," you are saying, "You are playing with good sound. . . . I like that."

Tone is either good or poor. Likewise, your child's tone will sound either good or poor, pleasing or irritating. While some music directors insist that learning rhythm is the most important element for a young musician to master, many music teachers insist that developing good tone is the most important early aspect of learning music. The fact is, because of changing body sizes, braces, and other factors, it may take years to develop consistently good tone. If your child can't seem to produce a good sound, don't despair. With persistence, it will come.

Parents: Go the Extra Mile for Good Tone

A Charting Exercise   Ask your child to chart on paper all the notes on his or her instrument that are "in tune" and "out of tune" as indicated by a tuner. Challenge your child to play those out-of-tune notes in tune. After documenting with a tuner all the notes on the instrument, give your child a special reward for playing a certain number of notes perfectly "in tune." You can easily check by having your child play the notes slowly while you watch the electronic tuner. The tuner will tell you if the notes are too high, too low, or perfect.

Record and Play Back   Create an opportunity where your child plays a note, or a group of notes, and you determine if the tone is good or poor. You can make a recording and play it back for discussion and further analysis.

Solo Practice   Encourage your child to play a solo that is slow and pretty while focusing on getting a beautiful, rich-sounding, sustained tone.

Listening   Take your family to a local concert and encourage your child to listen to how precisely and cleanly the soloist plays.

Practical Ideas for Helping Your Child Develop Outstanding Tone

❑ Slow Scales. Tell your child you'd like to hear notes on a scale played and held for approximately eight to sixteen seconds each. Encourage your child to focus and concentrate on producing the best possible sound while holding these notes.

❑ Warm Air. Wind players and brass players should blow using warm air. For example, when playing while using the syllable "he," cold air is used; however, when playing using the syllable "ho," warm air is used. This warm air tends to create a clear, open, and warm tone.

❑ Bow Placement. String players should concentrate on bow placement at or near the bridge. Discover where the note "rings out" and sounds the best, and play in this area.

❑ Compliment. If music sounds pleasing to your ear, say, "Your tone sounds great!"

❑ Long Tones. Ask your child to play each note of a scale or musical excerpt and hold each note for eight long, slow beats. Concentrate on producing the best sound possible while playing. This technique is similar to swinging a bat with a weight on it before going up to bat for real. It helps build strength and focus.

❑ Self-Check. Ask your child to perform a self-check. Check the following: body posture, placement on the chair, hands, arms, feet, and mouth.

❑ Double Play. Have your child play a small part of the music twice and try to make it sound better the second time.

❑ Listening. Play a recording of a professional musician for your child.

❑ Live Concert. Attend a live concert and make a comment about how good the tone sounds with professionals playing. Comments like "I wonder if you could sound like that" or "I bet you could sound that good" will be influential.

❑ Fill the Instrument. Tell wind players to take full, deep breaths, use warm air while blowing, and create a dark, beautiful sound.

❑ Review. Review, review, and review. Good tone is very important. Be sure your child regularly reviews the exact methods for producing good tone.

If something doesn't sound quite right, or perhaps is muffled or unclear, this is where you ask about tone. Comment on the tone, and encourage your budding musician to produce the best possible sound every day on every note. Use the term *tone* often with your child, especially after he or she performs for you.

INTONATION

The term *intonation* describes the quality of a particular sound or group of sounds, especially the sound produced when two or more instruments play simultaneously. For example, when two flutes play a duet together, they will have good or bad intonation. Specifically, when instruments play together and the sound quality is good, then the music is "in tune"—in other words, the intonation is good. Conversely, when a group of instruments are playing together and the sound is poor, the music is "out of tune," and the intonation is poor.

In band and orchestra settings, there are many possible variations of intonation—flute and clarinet, flute and sax, or flute and trumpet, to name a few. For the most part, you will not need to discuss this term, but after hearing a music concert, you may want to comment on it. If you say that the intonation was good, you are really telling your child, "Your sound was good and it matched the other players' sound." Good intonation is one sign of great music! For most musicians, it takes more time to learn to match other musicians' sounds than it does to learn how to play alone with good tone.

Practical Ideas for Helping Your Child Develop Good Intonation

When music is played by two or more people and you hear something strange inside the sound, such as a buzzing or waving sound (which may or may not be irritating to your ears), you might say, "Check your intonation on a few of the notes." Keep in mind that a beginning musician will most likely not know which notes are in error, so you may need to have your child play the song again and stop him or her at the proper moment in order to pinpoint the exact section that you feel needs work.

Purchase a tuner from your local store. By tuning the instrument, especially on certain key notes (which your music director or method book will show you), you can greatly improve the chance of your child playing in tune and thus being able to match fellow musicians. Eventually he or she will sound better and have more fun.

It's All Related

Technical and scientific descriptions of intonation are complicated. In a nutshell, poor intonation means that one instrument sounds too high or too low in relation to a second instrument.

In order to fix an inconsistency in conflicting sounds, players can easily adjust an instrument by lengthening or shortening it. For example, string players move the pegs and strings, and wind players move tuning slides, mouthpieces, or barrels. The result is that the musician can make the pitch of the instrument go higher or lower. Additionally, all wind players make their own intonation match another sound by adjusting their embouchure (mouth position) as they blow.

Are You Still Confused?

"Tone" and "intonation" are easily confused. Musicians with good tone will likely play "in tune" with other people, thus having good intonation. Players can achieve good intonation by "tuning up" with an electronic tuner. Instrument method books and music teachers can show your child how to do this. Musicians can also build good intonation by learning to listen and blend with their fellow musicians.

Tuning Point Equals Turning Point

Encourage your child to tune his or her instrument regularly. This will make a huge difference in his or her ability to play with good tone quality and in tune with other people. Learning how to tune an instrument marks a major turning point in your child's musical development. With good sound and good intonation, your child will be on the way to creating great music and will also have a lot more fun playing!

Musicians should strive to play with good tone and, by extension, good intonation. However, they must practice and learn these concepts in the music rehearsal and at home. Reminding your child about these critical concepts and emphasizing their importance sends an important message about music—you care about your child's success and you want him or her to improve. Try some of the ideas in the "Practical Ideas" section for developing better intonation.

THE LIFE OF A NOTE

Like a good story, a note has at least three parts: beginning (attack), middle (sustain), and end (release). How can you help your musician master all three parts? What do you say to your child and how can you guide him or her to new heights even if you don't play music or know nothing about your child's instrument?

Don't worry if you know little or nothing about music. This section will help you with these key points. We'll begin at the beginning—the attack.

Part One: The Attack

The beginning of a note is very important—after all, it's the first sound that you hear! Just as clear pronunciation in speech is important, so too is clear articulation in music.

Sometimes when your child plays a note, the beginning will not sound clear. There might be a pinched or scratchy sound, or perhaps the note won't sound at all. If you encounter this, try one of the following:

- For any instrument, first confirm that your child has good posture, is holding the instrument correctly, and has the proper position. If you're not sure exactly what is correct, carefully review the method book, where you will see pictures and helpful hints showing exactly what to do. You can also seek the assistance of a music teacher.
- For brass and woodwinds, ask your child to say the syllable "ta" or "da" several times. Next, see if he or she can produce a note on the instrument while using the syllable sound. For reed players, confirm that reeds are properly set on the mouthpiece.
- For strings, be sure that your child does not make the bow strike the string in a hard, heavy, or abrupt way. It is important to "bring out" or "pull out" the sound gently. Start from the string, not too heavily, with both hands working together—start a little bit above the string with a downward bow motion. While you pull the bow over the string, it actually scratches or bounces along the string and creates a sound. You will notice that with the right amount of

pressure of bow to string and the right speed of bow over string, a beautiful sound will emerge.

- For percussion, check your child's hand and stick positions. Next, ask your child to inhale and breathe while playing; this will make it easier to internalize the beat and start in time. For example, the child can inhale for two beats just before starting to play.

Part Two: Sustain

After the attack, the actual sound of the note (the tone) begins. I call this sound the *sustain*. A good sustain is warm and inviting, not harsh or crass, and it has direction and purpose. The sound should never be dull or stagnant. The sustain should move with the phrase, either leading into a high point or fading away into a soft conclusion.

If the notes your child plays seem "wavy" or generally unfocused, do not seem to move in any direction, or just sound bad, try some of the ideas below:

- For any instrument, check first to confirm that your child has good posture, is holding the instrument correctly, and has proper hand position. If you're not sure exactly what is correct, check the method book. If you're still not sure, seek assistance from the music director or a private teacher.
- For brass and woodwinds, getting enough air is critical. Encourage your child to take a deep, full breath before playing and to evenly space out the air while exhaling. It is important to avoid using up all the air at once. Have your child practice the breathing exercise described below.
- For strings, tell your child to hold the bow up and let the bow's weight bring out the sound as it is pulled out over the string. Once the sound is created, the motion should remain smooth.
- Percussionists usually need help playing drum rolls accurately. Encourage your child to play a roll very slowly and evenly—in a controlled and precise manner, repeating until he or she plays it precisely. Then have your child slowly speed up to the appropriate speed.

Breathing Exercise 8/4/2

A very effective and fun exercise for wind and string players is based on an 8/4/2 count. Ask your child to sit up properly and inhale evenly for eight counts, hold for eight counts, and exhale evenly for eight counts. Repeat this several times and then try it again using only four counts, and finally using only two counts. The key is "even in" and "even out." When your child can breath evenly, help him or her make the connection between breathing and producing the sound. Remember that a steady, even breath or arm movement is likely to produce a warm, pleasant sound. But an uneven, jerky breath or arm movement is likely to sound strange and unpleasant. Mastering the 8/4/2 exercise will help your child master musicianship.

Part Three: Release

The "release" of a note is the final part of the sound. For various reasons, some beginning musicians have tremendous difficulty in ending without a pinched or garbled sound. Although there are several schools of thought about how exactly to "release" a note, I suggest that beginning musicians try to end with a clear, yet precise and open sound. If you say "ma" out loud as in "mom-ma," you will notice that the ending "ma" sound is open and clean. If you can imagine your child producing the same type of open and clean sound, then you can easily begin to help him or her achieve it.

When and how do you cleanly stop a note? If your child is playing a note and sounds good only until the last moment (the release), try the following:

- For all players, check first to confirm that your child has good posture, is holding the instrument correctly, and has proper hand position.
- For brass and woodwinds, one of the most common problems is running out of air. This can be fixed by conserving air flow—by not using up all the air at once (practice the breathing exercise above). The second most common problem is that beginning musicians end with a crass "biting off" type of sound. This problem is easily fixed by saying the syllable "ma" as in "mom-ma." Ask your

child to focus on the long and open-ending "ahhh" sound and to try to replicate that open sound when playing. One way to practice is to slowly play one note at a time until each note ends correctly.

- For strings, fingers should release the sound at the right moment. In order to prepare for the release, it is important to count and co-ordinate (for example, "One, Two, Three, Release" or "One, Two, Three, Off").
- For percussion, your child may have few problems with releases. In order to prepare for the release, it is important to count (for example, "One, Two, Three, Release" or "One, Two, Three, Off").

TIME TO COUNT: TEMPO AND RHYTHM

Playing with the proper *tempo* and *rhythm* can help your child sound better, play more expressively, and have more fun. Because both terms are related to movement, they can be easily confused—until now.

Tempo

In the good old rock-and-roll days, a piece of music would start out like this: "A-one, a-two, a-one-two-three." The group would start to play, and the tempo would be set. Come to think of it, they still do that a lot, don't they? In any event, the tempo is the speed of a piece. Much like your heartbeat, tempo in music is usually consistent and doesn't change much. Imagine the sound your beating heart makes as it works: thub-dub, thub-dub, thub-dub. The tempo your heart creates is consistent and predictable—and so is the tempo in a piece of music. Once it starts, it continues, and you can accurately tap your toe to the beat.

Tempo in sheet music is often noted in the upper left corner at the beginning of the piece. You basically only need to know three tempos—slow (walking tempo), medium (jogging tempo), or fast (running tempo). Sometimes tempo is notated in relation to the number of beats per minute. You might encounter, for example, a quarter note equaling 120. At the beginning, you needn't worry about this too much. Later on, as you and your child become more familiar with how to use the metronome, these numbers will become clearer to you. For now, here is a short exercise to help with tempo:

Check the beginning of your child's music in the upper left-hand corner of the page. Nine out of ten times, the tempo marking is written down. If it is written in a foreign language, look up the meaning in your child's method book. Even if your child has to start by practicing slowly, this will tell you about how fast the piece should be played.

Clap your hands as your child plays. If your child is playing a piece and it sounds "off," there is likely a tempo issue. Try clapping your hands much like you would at a rock-and-roll concert (on the beat)—this clapping may help your child maintain a consistent tempo.

Rhythm

Rhythm is a collection of recurring musical patterns and sounds. Repeat to yourself three times, "Row, row, row your boat." After that, say to yourself, "da, da, da DI da." Did you notice a pattern? That pattern is rhythm. Good rhythm almost begs you to hear more. It's like a sentence that must be completed. Did you find yourself wanting to finish the musical idea and say, "gently down the stream"? Part of your child's job in learning how to play an instrument is to find the beat (rhythm) in each piece and stick to it.

In addition to developing good tone and playing correct notes, having a sense of rhythm is vitally important for a beginning musician. It is one of the basic building blocks required for becoming a master musician, and it can take effort to develop. Although some music teachers insist that tone is the most important first element to learn in music, many other teachers believe that developing good rhythm is a hallmark of future success. Here are some ideas for helping with rhythm:

- Slow down. If your child does not know a rhythm or phrase in the music, slowing the tempo down can make it easier to learn the correct rhythm.
- Subdivide. Encourage your child to subdivide the beats in order to focus more on counting. Instead of counting 1-2-3-4, try this: 1-AND-2-AND-3-AND-4-AND.

- Style check. Check the style of music your child plays. It most likely will either be classical or jazz, and therefore it should be either "straight" or "laid back." Both styles have distinct differences. Over time, as your musician learns to recognize and accentuate them, you'll hear better and more convincing music.

Parents: Go the Extra Mile for Rhythm and Tempo

- Have some fun. Clap your hands to the consistent tempo and beat of rock-and-roll music. If you can, try clapping on the off beat. Clap your hands or snap your fingers to the beat as your child plays for you.
- Go to a live jazz concert and ask your child to figure out who really keeps the tempo.
- Try this little challenge: See if you or your child can tap three beats in one hand and two beats in the other hand at the same time! Hint: you may want to use some math to figure out exactly where the beats should sound. Next, see if you can detect the unique rhythm that emerges. Finally, see if you can alternate hands. If you are really feeling adventurous, try tapping three beats in one hand while tapping four in the other. Remember this is as much a math challenge as a music challenge. Good luck!

CONCEPT CHECK—BUILDING BASICS

Do you understand how to support your child and inspire musicality? Do you understand what you need to do in order to critique yet motivate? The following checklist will help you answer these questions. Remember, if you miss any of these questions, go back and find out exactly how to do it correctly—or ask a professional or private teacher. Check the appropriate boxes below:

Do you . . .

❑ insist on correct hand, mouth, and body position?
❑ encourage practice of long, slow tones?

❑ compliment when you hear good tone or intonation?

❑ encourage self-review and analysis after playing?

❑ support listening to live concerts and professional musicians?

❑ insist on crisp, precise attacks?

❑ compliment your child when a note is sustained with sensitivity and control?

❑ stop and note the parts of a sound that are unclear or pinched?

❑ tap your foot lightly as your child performs?

❑ give positive comments about rhythm and style?

· 7 ·

Focus on Musicality

Ah, music. A magic beyond all we do here!

—J. K. Rowling, *Harry Potter and the Sorcerer's Stone*

*D*ynamics are changes in volume or loudness of music. When starting out in music, your child will learn to play loudly or softly, depending upon what the music calls for. This is called dynamics. Using dynamics correctly will enable your child to express and sculpt one very important part of music: the musical phrase, or sentence. The challenge is to use dynamics to make the music expressive enough to communicate with the audience. Dynamics should be an extension of the player's emotions.

Dynamic contrasts make music interesting to hear and fun to play! The most common terms related to dynamics are listed in table 7.1. You will find some of these terms in most pieces of music. When used correctly, these simple terms guide your child to make music more expressive and more exciting. Notice that they are all based on variations of loud and soft and are easily understood by nonmusicians.

Table 7.1. Dynamic Terms

Symbol	Term	Meaning
pp	Pianissimo	Very Soft
p	Piano	Soft
mp	Mezzo Piano	Medium Soft
mf	Mezzo Forte	Medium Loud
f	Forte	Loud
ff	Fortissimo	Very Loud

ENCOURAGE A WIDE RANGE OF DYNAMICS

Ask for Different Dynamic Levels

Long pieces of music are usually numbered or lettered at major sections. Ask your child to play the different musical sections at a different dynamic levels.

Use Constructive Comments

As your child plays at dynamic levels, listen for improvements in sound. Comment on what you think and feel.

Encourage Expression

Encourage your child to include dynamic expression throughout the music in order to make it sound more dramatic and exciting. Keep in mind that playing softly is just as important as playing loudly. Also note that music often has only a few dynamic markings written down; it is the responsibility of the player to add them as necessary.

Play the Opposite, Loudly

If your child is having difficulty playing something softly, ask him or her to play it loudly at first and then get gradually softer.

Play the Opposite, Softly

If your child is having difficulty playing something loudly, ask him or her to play it softly at first and then get gradually louder.

Should My Child Practice Loudly or Softly?

Tell your child to try playing a loud section of music softly while maintaining the correct style, phrasing, and tone. Then have him or her try it again at the correct dynamic level.

Many beginning musicians play too loudly because they haven't yet developed skills that allow them to play softly with confidence and musical expression. Encourage your musician to play a phrase as beautifully and delicately at a soft dynamic level as at a loud dynamic level. Here are some slightly more advanced activities:

Go to a Professional Concert

At the concert, see if you can detect the dynamic changes from loud (*forte*) to soft (*piano*). Next, listen for changes that are only medium loud (*mezzo forte*) to medium soft (*mezzo piano*). Can you detect dynamic changes that are even more refined than what you have already heard?

Play a Miniconcert

Encourage your child to play a miniconcert for you. Have him or her play the piece at one dynamic level and then again at the opposite dynamic level.

Memorize and Play

Ask your child to memorize a favorite song and then try to play it for you demonstrating basic dynamic levels and contrasts.

STACCATO AND LEGATO MAKE STYLE

A staccato sound can be thought of as detached sound, while a legato sound can be thought of as connected sound. Have you ever heard someone playing "Chopsticks" on the piano? That is an example of staccato. "Silent Night," on the other hand, is played legato. Jump-rope rhymes are staccato. Lullabies are legato. Most people, especially beginning musicians, commonly refer to staccato and legato as short and long. In order to master music, your child will need to be able to play both styles accurately.

Let's fool around with "Happy Birthday to You" for a minute. When you usually sing it, it sounds legato, and you can tell that the first two lines are separate musical phrases: "Happy Birthday to You, Happy Birthday to You." Singing it staccato ("Hap! py! birth! day! to! you! Hap! py! birth! day! to! you!") takes away the feelings and makes the words sound meaningless. A young musician's goal is to figure out the best style for each melody played.

The challenge a young musician faces is to play all the notes in a musical phrase consistently and with the correct style. Can you imagine playing a long, slow, sad song using the incorrect style? Instead of connected sounds, you end up with detached short sounds—not a good idea and not exactly a great musical experience for the audience.

The challenge is met when the musician plays with sensitivity, constant listening, and constant adjusting. These skills can be acquired with patience, effort, and encouragement. Encourage your child to develop and express a unique musical voice when learning to play short and long.

How Short Is Short?

Many musicians play staccato in a way that results in extremely short playing —to the point where the note actually sounds chopped off. Although the notes are indeed short and separated, this is incorrect musicianship, and it sounds bad. Very few pieces of music call for chopped-off sound.

How short is appropriate? The correct length to play a note is largely based on the style of the music. This requires knowledge that can be gained over time with experimentation, trial and error, and experience. One of the best ways to learn about appropriate lengths of notes is to listen to professional recordings.

The important thing to remember is that music should have grace and elegance. Notes that are too short or too long will change the style and mood of the piece. Gradually, as your child's skills and tastes become more refined, he or she will be able to alter the length of the notes as necessary and desired.

Parents: Go the Extra Mile with Staccato and Legato

- Play Legato. Encourage your child to play an entire section or piece legato.

- Play Staccato. Encourage your child to play an entire section or piece staccato.
- Play Plain. If the sound is not clear or consistent, ask your child to play the piece without staccato or legato—just play it plain.
- Encourage Stylistic Development. Encourage your child to explore playing music with different styles of long and short notes so that the music sounds appealing and interesting.

Should My Child Practice Fast or Slow?

Tell your child to practice a fast piece of music slowly while maintaining correct style and phrasing. Then he or she can gradually speed up until reaching the correct tempo.

RAISING THE BAR: MASTERING TECHNIQUE

You have probably heard a lot of talk about "technique," but what exactly is it? Technique in music refers to the command that a musician has over the fundamental musical concepts we have discussed, including tone, tempo, notes, and expression. One of the biggest challenges for your musician will be to take each of the concepts, focus on them one at a time during practice, and ultimately put all of the pieces together. When your child is frustrated, encourage him or her to remember this: in order to become an expressive artist, you must strive to learn a little bit every day. Master musicians have complete control over all fundamental areas of their art, and your child should strive for this control, too.

You will encourage good technical development by having your child master the material in the method book. There are many outstanding method books in print, so if you are unsure about the appropriateness of one versus another, call your music director or local music store for a reference.

The two areas that have the biggest effect on your child's technical and musical development are practice and hard work! Part II of this book, "Practice Makes Perfect," offers useful advice on how your child can get the most out of practice time.

One of the great things about music is that it helps develop both character and technique—at the same time. In fact, they seem to develop hand in hand! Beyond helping musicians play the right notes, count the tempo, produce good tone, and create meaningful and expressive playing, working on technique reinforces positive character traits like hard work, goal setting, prioritizing, and thinking globally rather than locally. Technique and character seem to complement each other. That is why character development and technique training are so important—they both help to create the types of citizens that we value in society, in our schools, and in our workplaces.

MUSICALITY CONCEPT QUIZ

Do you understand how to support your child and inspire musicality? Do you understand how and what you need to do in order to critique yet motivate your musician? The following list will help you answer these questions. Remember, if you miss any of these questions, go back and find out exactly how to do it correctly, or ask your band director or a private teacher for help.

Do you . . .

- ❑ encourage correct use of dynamics for musical effect?
- ❑ encourage use of dynamics on melodies, solos, and long notes?
- ❑ compliment your child when you hear dynamics being used?
- ❑ encourage crisp, clear sound via staccato and legato?
- ❑ insist on clear, precise attacks?
- ❑ encourage mastery of the instrument through good technique?
- ❑ encourage good practice habits that will lead to outstanding technique?
- ❑ insist on improving technical areas that may be below par?
- ❑ know and follow the National Standards for Music Education?
- ❑ recognize if your music group meets or exceeds the recommended proficiency in the standards?

THE NATIONAL STANDARDS

Nationally recognized music standards created by the National Association for Music Education (MENC) promote essential elements of musical development for students in kindergarten through twelfth grade. They are important because they establish clear benchmarks that allow professionals and "civilians" alike the ability to gauge the success of a student and school. National standards set high expectations for all states, schools, and music organizations to work toward. Below is a list of the standards; see www .menc.org/publication/books/standards.htm and artsedge.kennedy-center .org/teach/standards.cfm for more information.

The National Standards

1. Singing, alone and with others, a varied repertoire of music.
2. Performing on instruments, alone and with others, a varied repertoire of music.
3. Improvising melodies, variations, and accompaniments.
4. Composing and arranging music within specified guidelines.
5. Reading and notating music.
6. Listening to, analyzing, and describing music.
7. Evaluating music and music performances.
8. Understanding relationships between music, the other arts, and disciplines outside the arts.
9. Understanding music in relation to history and culture.

STATE STANDARDS

Many states have adapted, enhanced, or developed their own statewide music standards. Some standards are very similar to the national standards; however, some are quite different. You can find your state's music standards at www.educationworld.com/arts/.

WHAT SHOULD I DO WITH
MUSIC STANDARDS INFORMATION?

Talk with your music director and school administrators. Confirm that they are developing music programs that are based on the standards. Figure out ways that you can help your child to develop further based on the standards.

PARENTS: GO THE EXTRA MILE WITH THE NATIONAL STANDARDS

National Standards

Encourage your child to make a list of the National Standards for Music Education and the ways that your music program utilizes them. Does your local music program utilize all the standards or only some? If you think your program may be lacking in an area, see if you can find out why. Perhaps there is great opportunity to help build or develop your child, your local music group, and your community.

Standards in School

Meet with your school administrator and confirm that your music program is aligned with the national standards. Meet with your music director and ask if there is a way that you can help him or her develop a better music program based on the national standards.

Demonstration

Bring your family to a concert and go backstage. Ask one of the musicians (preferably one who plays your child's instrument) to demonstrate an excerpt or two from the concert music.

Play Dates

Encourage your child to invite friends over to play music together. Music can be a lot of fun when played in a group—especially for a beginner. Together, children can work up music for a miniconcert, and during their preparation you might comment on their hard work, commitment, and outstanding tone and intonation.

Private Lessons

Find a private teacher who plays your child's instrument, and sign up for private lessons.

Purchase Music

Purchase different types and styles of music for your child to play. Solo, duet, trio, and chamber music books are good choices.

TONY'S TOP TEN

1. Select a good-quality instrument that you are sincerely interested in learning to play.
2. Practice regularly. Set a special time aside each day to practice in a quiet, well-lit room equipped with a music stand, a chair, and a pencil for marking work and progress.
3. If at all possible, study with a private teacher.
4. Practice smart. Decide which type of practice session is the best for you—Thirty-Minute, Sixty-to-Ninety-Minute, Marathon, or 70/30—and then use it.
5. Practice with a purpose and a goal. Break sections into small parts and learn them.
6. All great musicians play with outstanding tone, intonation, tempo, rhythm, and dynamic control. So should you!
7. Good staccato and legato playing takes time to develop. Start right now.
8. Become familiar with the National Standards for Music Education —they cover all your bases as a musician.
9. Work hard, never give up, and be, the best you can be!
10. Have fun! Take pride in your accomplishments. Set aside a few minutes of each practice to show off for yourself or others. Perform for other people and ask for their honest opinions.

• *Appendix A* •

College and Beyond

$\mathcal{E}$ntrance into college seems to be getting more difficult each year. Standards remain high, and competition among the thousands of applicants continues to increase. But for those who are interested in entering college to study music, there is indeed a method for gaining a coveted acceptance letter. For those who are determined, there are a few "tricks" that I will explain in this appendix. I will also discuss what colleges hope to see from their applicants, what types of music programs colleges offer, and what it takes to win an acceptance letter (and possibly a scholarship) into your school of choice.

DO COLLEGES NEED MUSICIANS?

Yes, they do! Many colleges and universities develop and nurture performing arts programs that include band or orchestra. These schools continually admit musicians to study, play, and perform music, but because students are graduating every year, music programs need new students to replenish vacated positions. Schools have learned that they must offer attractive financial aid to help lure students into their programs. Furthermore, many music programs offer scholarships for exceptionally talented musicians. Believe it or not, some schools do not even require you to be a music major to receive music scholarship money.

Every college program—including sports, academics, sciences, art, and music—must fill every team position, every seat in the classroom, and every music chair with a balanced and diverse group of people. Because of finances, social trends, and a host of other circumstances, schools are not always able to enroll enough of the people they are hoping to attract. Imagine having a football team, but not having any quarterbacks enroll. Can you imagine an orchestra without violinists? Or a band with no trumpets? Music departments need new musicians to fill open positions because if too many violin players graduate and not enough new players come in, then the orchestra will end up unbalanced, or worse—there will be no orchestra at all! And this is where your child can benefit from being able to fill one of those empty seats.

A Truly Inspiring Story

A student who recently graduated from an Ivy League college shares her personal story on music and success:

I am congenitally blind. I have been totally blind since birth and have never had any functional vision, but I recently graduated from an Ivy League school, and if I can do it so can your child!

One of my favorite activities was participating in my college orchestra and band. Despite having every excuse not to participate and succeed, I persevered. In fact, I even won a solo competition against fellow undergraduates. I studied hard, developed myself, and, importantly, never gave up. There is a simple key idea that has propelled me to the point where I am, and it is something that you can help your child achieve too—hard work.

I want you to know that everyone has challenges. Some people have weight problems, others have work-ethic problems, but we all face challenges; it's how we deal with these challenges that makes us a success!

It doesn't matter how you feel, you just have to keep going and focus on things that you need to accomplish.

WHAT CAN PARENTS DO?

Many schools have a premier music group, such as a marching band, jazz band, or symphony orchestra. Each group needs musicians to play and perform at important school events and ceremonies (including sporting events and graduation). You would be surprised at how many schools have these important, highly visible programs—and are looking for musicians right now, even as you read this book!

Parents should call their colleges of interest and find out what traditionally is the most desired or sought-after instrument. Many schools tend to have chronic deficiencies in their enrollment, particularly in certain instrument categories. Parents should also inquire about anticipated openings —perhaps the school your child wants to attend already has five oboe players, and they do not anticipate needing any for the next several years. If your child plays the oboe, it would almost seem silly to put all your eggs in this basket!

Parents should also consider meeting with a college counselor and music teacher at the school of interest. By inquiring in advance and meeting with key people, you give yourself a head start on the difficult entrance process. Why wait for them to call you (they usually don't), when you can call them? Get your child's name out there in front of the regular pool of applicants, and sell yourself to the music program *before* final decisions are made.

CHECKLIST FOR PARENTS

❑ Plan for private lessons. Nearly every successful college student and professional musician has had a private teacher in the middle/high school and college years.
❑ Consider having your child study privately with the head music teacher of the school that he or she wishes to attend. Private teachers are usually in a very good position to recommend you directly

into the music department and, by extension, into the college. Additionally, contact music department heads and focus on the actions that will result in winning scholarship money. Find out scholarship audition dates and requirements, including solo literature and scale requirements.

- ❑ Be proactive in learning about colleges. Tour your prospective music schools early. Meet the music counselor, administrator, and special private teacher. Find out how admission decisions are made and how to win scholarship money.
- ❑ Encourage your child to make a solid yearlong commitment to learning a new instrument—including summer.
- ❑ Encourage your child to earn the highest GPA reasonably possible.
- ❑ Create an environment for your child that encourages extensive performance opportunities.
- ❑ Help your child become an "expert" on at least one instrument.
- ❑ Decide if a conservatory or a liberal arts learning environment is best.
- ❑ Encourage your child to have a backup plan—maybe a music education minor.
- ❑ Save early, plan early.

THE COST OF COLLEGE

If you plan to send your child to college, you need to know that the cost of sending a child to college is rising and is expected to continue rising. In 2000, the average cost of room, board, and tuition at a four-year public college was around $11,338 per year, while a four-year private college cost roughly $24,946 per year. However, twenty years later (2018), the same education (predicted to rise 5 percent annually), will cost approximately $27,291 and $57,158, respectively.[1] College is clearly an expensive proposition!

It's easy to see that if your child is going to college in five or ten years you may want to plan now, as costs will be high—very high! So how is selecting the right instrument related? Certain instruments are chronically underrepresented in many colleges and music schools; I call these instruments "green instruments" because a student who plays one of them well may see a lot of money in the form of scholarships and grants. The "green instruments" list below shows which instruments are sought after. If your child plays one of these instruments well, you may benefit significantly by paying thousands of dollars less in yearly tuition. By having this information in advance and planning early, you can give your child a distinct advantage by having him or her study one of these instruments.

The "Green Instruments"
- Strings
  - Viola
  - Bass
- Woodwinds
  - Oboe
  - Bassoon
- Brass
  - French horn
  - Trombone
  - Euphonium
  - Tuba

STUDYING MUSIC IN COLLEGE

There are several ways students can study music in college. First, students can enroll in a class for fun. This is good for the hobbyist and the person who appreciates participating in music. For the serious music student and the one who wants to pursue music or music education as a profession, there are two primary types of study: a music (or music education) major and a music (or music education) minor. The decision of whether to be a music major or music minor may influence whether your child gets into his or her first-choice college. This is something you will need to determine and consider *before* applying.

THE MUSIC MAJOR

A music major primarily studies music and music performance. Typically, this student will devote a good deal of time to learning a specific instrument or skill (for example, violin or music teaching). Most music major programs are intensive and are designed to educate in the many different areas of music while focusing on one key specialty, such as percussion. Music education majors learn how to teach music.

Advantages of Majoring in Music

One of the biggest advantages of majoring in music is that music majors obtain a degree that is very focused, and therefore musicians have the opportunity to become "experts" in their area of specialty. This allows them to potentially be more competitive in the music industry upon graduation and therefore may increase their ability to secure work in the industry.

Disadvantages of Majoring in Music

Studying only one specific skill can be a handicap, especially when entering the music industry. If you are unable to find work in your specific field, a finely tuned and specific degree may actually hurt, particularly in a weak job market.

A Backup Plan for the Music Major

The general economic outlook for musicians is not rosy. Artists in general have a tremendous amount of competition for relatively few jobs. Additionally, except for a few "superstar" performers, salaries for performing musicians have remained comparatively low for the past few decades. "Performing artists continue to dedicate themselves to their art despite the fact that their pay and job security have scarcely improved since the 1970s."[2] In comparison with workers in general, performing artists typically earn less, work fewer weeks, and face higher unemployment than professionals with comparable education levels.[3]

For these reasons, a good backup plan is wise. Probably the best option for most people who intend to work in a music-related field is to study music as a major and then obtain extra certifications and credentials in a related field. For example, a student who plays the flute may want to become certified to teach music at either the elementary or secondary level.

THE MUSIC MINOR

A music minor primarily studies something besides music and then studies music as a secondary field. For example, a student might study medicine and declare music as a minor. Many students who declare music as a minor do not intend to work in the music field; rather, they enjoy music for its own sake and want to excel in it.

Advantages of a Music Minor

Most people who study music as a music minor recognize the difficult realities of working in the music industry, and they want to improve their music skills. These students want to augment their current education, and they do this by studying something they enjoy. Another type of student who declares a music minor is the music major who wants to learn a related instrument in order to become more competitive.

Disadvantages of a Music Minor

Besides potentially costing more in time, money, and energy, there are no disadvantages to obtaining a music minor.

PROGRAMS OF STUDY

There are two basics styles of music education in college: conservatory and liberal arts. Before applying to a school, your child should consider which program is most suitable. Most schools focus exclusively on one style, so deciding which style to pursue will dictate the specific school that your child will attend.

The Music School/Conservatory Approach

The conservatory approach is highly specific and targeted. Although most programs using this method also offer writing and other academic courses, the primary focus is on music. Some people equate the conservatory style of intense music education with a specialty trade school, where students are immersed in their specific field and quickly learn the craft and technique that will help them succeed. An example of a person studying under the conservatory approach is someone studying violin at the Juilliard School.

Liberal Arts

A liberal arts approach offers a music degree similar to that of the conservatory; however, it encourages the student to study other subjects, such as math, language, science, and history. An example of a person studying under the liberal arts approach is a person studying at the University of California, Los Angeles.

WHAT ARE COLLEGES LOOKING FOR?

Basically, all schools want the best students and the best musicians. That said, they are really looking for one important thing, the students who they think will successfully graduate. They strive to figure out how to obtain a high number of graduates in relation to the number of students admitted.

Musicians apply to top music schools through an application process that typically includes the four key elements listed below.

Audition

After completing the initial application, most schools require a live audition. As you can imagine, this audition is very important and should be performed as well as possible.

Grades

Grades are always an important factor in your overall application. As might be expected, the higher the grades, the better the chance of admission! Students should strive to earn high grades even in classes that they may feel are unrelated to their music career. After all, when it comes down to a tie, the person with higher grades may win!

Standardized Tests

SAT or ACT test scores tend to be more important in liberal arts schools than in conservatories. Check with your schools of interest to see which test they require. A musician should strive to obtain the highest scores possible on these tests. As with grades, when it comes down to a tie, the person with the higher test score may win!

Other Important Essentials

Some other key areas that may help your child's college application include leadership, community service, the essay, and personal recommendations. Any of these areas may give your child just the credentials that an application review committee is looking for. Remember, when things get down to the final decision, the student with the best credentials is most likely to gain entrance—so always encourage your child to do his or her best!

THE ARTS AND THE UNIVERSITY

Representatives of major universities offered these comments on the role of the arts in the admission process when Tom Duffy of Yale University queried them in 1992 (www.duffymusic.com/articles/cmea.html). Excellence in music is a common denominator at many schools. As you can see from these comments, musical expertise is one factor that can boost an applicant's chances of acceptance into a top university.

Yale University

Worth David, Dean of Undergraduate Admissions:

> Qualifications for admission to Yale College include not only the reasonably well-defined areas of academic achievement and special skill in non-academic areas, but also the less tangible qualities of capacity for involvement, commitment, and personal growth. The arts offer remarkable opportunities for the exercise of these qualities. The highly skilled artist, the student whose intellectual interests include close study of the arts, and the many applicants who demonstrate motivation and the willingness to extend their reach through participation in the arts, all promise to enhance the quality of life at Yale.

Harvard University

William R. Fitzsimmons, Dean of Admissions:

> The arts are clearly an integral part of life at Harvard and Radcliffe, important for their value to the college environment and also for the potential they provide for lifelong enrichment. In addition to academic criteria, therefore, we always consider extracurricular talents and personal strengths when we evaluate a candidate's credentials. We look for students whose previous participation in the arts shows that they can make a substantial contribution to our community.

University of Virginia

John A. Blackburn, Dean of Admissions:

> The founder of this university, Thomas Jefferson, was an avid musician himself, and his influence can be seen today in the strength of the offerings in music, drama, art studio, history of art, and also architecture. This university seeks students who have solid backgrounds in English, math, science, history, and foreign languages. In addition, we look for students who have well-developed talents in the arts, for we know that they add a richness to our student body. They enhance the quality of life for all of our students and faculty at the University of Virginia.

University of Michigan

Richard H. Shaw Jr., Director of Admissions:

> Intellectual leaders from Plato to the present have recognized the importance of the arts to a thriving civilization. The University of Michigan joins in recommending the arts because of their humanizing influences, their demands for self-discipline, their abilities to evoke idealistic dreams that transcend everyday issues, their effectiveness in reflecting the achievements of diverse peoples, and their capacities to stimulate that most important of all intellectual abilities: creativity. Perhaps in no past era of our increasingly global civilization have these qualities been more sorely needed than they are today. The University of Michigan in Ann Arbor is a community rich in varied artistic achievements, and we are especially pleased to consider applicants whose backgrounds synchronize with artistic values.

University of California, Los Angeles (UCLA)

Vu Tran, Director of Undergraduate Admissions and Relations with Schools:

> As one of America's premier universities for teaching, research, and service, UCLA conducts a comprehensive review of applicants to all programs. In the selection process, we define merits beyond the standard academic elements, which include but are not limited to grades, test scores, or academic subjects completed. UCLA values students with special talents and/or accomplishments in extracurricular activities. Students who can demonstrate their skills and achievements as accomplished musicians or artists would definitely enhance their chance for admissions in all majors.
>
> Those students who are interested in majoring in music can select from three areas: music (performance, education and composition), jazz, and ethnomusicology. In the first two, a high degree of performance skill is necessary for admission. For ethnomusicology, the university is seeking curious students with a broad interest in music making from a variety of traditions and with a desire to enrich their knowledge in the unparalleled environment for study of the arts that UCLA offers. Beyond the auditions, all prospective music, jazz, and ethnomusicology majors must meet the minimum admissions requirements of the University of California. (*This quote was obtained directly through Vu Tran's office.*)

NOTES

1. *Financial Planning for College*, Pamphlet 510L, U.S. Department of the Treasury, 2001.

2. Kevin F. McCarthy, *The Performing Arts in a New Era* (Santa Monica, Calif.: Rand, 2001), xix.

3. McCarthy, *Performing Arts*, 42.

• *Appendix B* •

Private Lessons

$\mathscr{I}$can't overemphasize the distinct advantage of taking private lessons. I have yet to meet a professional musician who has not had many years of private lessons. For this reason, I recommend that all students enroll in private lessons as early as possible. Private lessons will dramatically improve your child's chances of gaining entrance into college to study music or becoming a professional musician.

Taking music lessons from a private teacher requires a significant commitment of time and money, but in order for a child to progress quickly and become above average, lessons are essential. Musicians who move to the front of the pack will almost always have a special private teacher behind them showing them shortcuts and helping them with the learning process.

During private lessons, students can work on areas of playing that may not be practical during a large band or orchestra class. Students can also learn special techniques and strategies that will help them improve. Finally, they can study unique areas and ways of thinking that can help them develop advanced music-making skills.

Private music study can even help your child in nonmusical studies. One study showed that music students who studied privately for two or more years performed significantly better on the ninth-grade composite mathematics portions of the Iowa Test of Basic Skills![1]

THE PIED PIPER

Juanita was very excited about playing the flute solo. Bright, energetic, and intelligent, she had a natural gift for music and an intrinsic understanding of good sound. I called her the "Pied Piper" because she sounded so good. Music was her main school activity. Although Juanita didn't have a private flute teacher, she still wanted to play a flute solo at the spring concert. The problem was that she didn't know what to play. She bought flute solo books, but she didn't know exactly what makes a good solo or how to select one.

I suggested that Juanita and her mother call Julie, a local flute specialist and professional musician, and ask her for advice and take lessons. After talking with Julie and learning how much a private teacher helps, Juanita was able to buy the appropriate solo music that would challenge her, yet be interesting. Excitedly, Juanita also agreed to take weekly flute lessons.

With her private teacher, Juanita blossomed and became incredibly motivated! She practiced daily and talked to the other students about her private lessons and how much fun she was having learning new music and new techniques. She even showed off before class by playing solos and fast flourishes up and down the range of her instrument. She blossomed into an absolutely fantastic soloist. And when the big spring concert arrived, Juanita was able to play a very difficult flute solo with all of her friends accompanying her.

Juanita's solo was well received, and she moved up to the next level—she became an artist.

FINDING A TEACHER

If you want to enroll your child in private lessons, look for a specialist who plays the instrument that your child plays. The music teacher at your child's school can probably provide you with names of some of the best teachers in your area. You could also call your local music store or your local university, look on the Internet, or check your local phone book for names of qualified teachers with good references and training.

THE ROLE OF PARENTS

I encourage parents to sit in on all private lessons if possible. By doing this, you will know exactly what values and techniques the teacher is trying to instill. You can then encourage and promote further development of those characteristics at home. Even if you know little or nothing about music, your child will benefit from knowing that you are interested in his or her musical growth and success.

If you or your child is having trouble knowing what exactly to practice, you can ask your child's private teacher for advice on how to organize your time and your goals. The private teacher can also help your child develop specific practice skills to use when working on particularly challenging pieces.

SUMMER MUSIC CAMP

Music camp is not necessary, but it is a lot of fun! Summer vacation is the best time for children to recharge their mental energy, and it is also a great time to enjoy music making. It can also be a helpful alternative for parents who cannot afford regular private lessons but who do want to provide some music enrichment outside what's offered during the school day.

In a summer music camp, your child will be able to experience music in a special way that is impossible during the daily school schedule. Half-day camps, which usually last about four or five hours a day, are one option. There are also full-day sleepover camps that can last for several days or weeks.

NOTE

1. Joyce M. Cheek and Lyle R. Smith, "Music Training and Mathematics Achievement of Ninth Graders," *Adolescence* 34, no. 136 (Winter 1999): 759–61.

• *Appendix C* •

Instrument Nuts and Bolts

*T*his section includes descriptions of each instrument family (brass, woodwind, strings, and percussion) and provides information on specific instruments your child may be interested in playing. You can consult this section to learn more about how each instrument sounds, how to care for an instrument, and how to decide if an instrument is right for you and your child. When deciding, be sure to check with your school's music teacher to find out what instruments are taught to beginners. Note also that the physical descriptions of body types are not absolute. For example, though a large body size is very helpful for a tuba player, there have been success- ful tuba students who are small in stature.

You will also find a list of model numbers that I recommend if you decide to purchase any of these instruments. Please note that these are only recommendations; your music director may have different prefer- ences. Keep in mind also that you may be able to borrow an instrument— particularly a large or expensive instrument like a bassoon, string bass, tuba, or bass clarinet—from the school.

Near the end of each instrument description, you will find a list of items your child will need in order to play well. Most of the supplies listed are available at your local music store. No matter what instrument you choose, consider providing recordings of famous musicians playing the in- strument and a challenging solo book to inspire your child to achieve even greater levels. A computer or stereo that can record and play back sound and video, along with a metronome and tuner, can also help your child.

In addition to the items listed above, there are thousands of optional items, including carrying cases, instrument floor stands, and special chairs. There is also every imaginable music-related product, including stickers, shirts, posters, key chains, and books. You may want to consider giving an optional item as a gift. And don't forget that these optional items work well as incentives and motivators!

MEET THE BRASS FAMILY

Brass instruments (trumpet, French horn, trombone, baritone horn, euphonium, tuba) are primarily made from soft metals, including nickel and brass. Brass instruments are often referred to as brasswinds because they require air (wind) to produce sound. Players produce sound by pressing the lips together and pushing air through them, resulting in a vibration or "buzz." The vibrating lips actually create the sound. When the vibrating lips are put into the mouthpiece, the instrument amplifies the sound and focuses it in a specific direction.

Cleaning Brass Instruments

Warm, moist air passes through the instrument's cool metal, causing condensation (or "spit") to form on the inside of the instrument. In addition to opening the "spit valve" so that condensation can drain out, players should also regularly pull out tuning slides to empty the instrument of excess condensation. This helps reduce or eliminate mold, mildew, bacteria, and unusual deposits that cause an unpleasant smell to develop inside the instrument.

How Often?   Remove condensation daily. Clean the mouthpiece once a week. Do a major cleaning of the whole instrument once a month. Have a professional music repair person clean the instrument and give it a tune-up each year before school starts.

What Do We Need?   For major cleaning, you need water, soap, an instrument snake (a thin, flexible rod with bristles), valve oil, slide grease, a towel, and an instrument cleaning brush.

How Long Does It Take? Smaller instruments can be cleaned in approximately thirty minutes; larger instruments may take over an hour.

What Do We Do? Thoroughly run water (preferably warm) through the instrument along with a few drops of mild liquid hand or dish soap. Use an instrument snake to loosen unwanted material originating from food eaten before playing from the inside of your instrument.

After completely flushing all soap and unwanted material from the instrument, carefully lubricate valves with valve oil and slides with slide grease.

The most common area of unwanted buildup is the mouthpiece. "Snake out" or "brush out" the mouthpiece once a week. A cotton swab is also useful in cleaning out the mouthpiece.

Remember that a good-smelling instrument is more fun to play. Encourage your child to brush his or her teeth before playing. This will have a tremendous impact on the cleanliness and smell of the instrument.

Notes on the Trumpet

With a long, metallic curved tube and a bell that faces forward, the trumpet is easily held with two hands. It consists of three valves and is the shortest and, therefore, the highest-sounding instrument in the brass family. Musicians play the trumpet by tightening and loosening their lips (embouchure) while pressing the valves.

Unique Facts The trumpet is a very old instrument. In fact, there are two trumpets preserved in the Cairo Museum of Egypt that came from the ancient tomb of King Tutankhamen. The trumpet has been used to communicate over battlefields for centuries.

Is the Trumpet Right for Us? Trumpet players need teeth that are basically straight, lips that are not large, and hands that are large enough to cover the valves. Players should enjoy higher sounds, melodic lines, and loud music.

What Supplies Will We Need? You'll need a soft cleaning cloth, valve oil, a straight mute, a mouthpiece cleaning brush, slide grease, a pencil, a method book, and a music stand.

Which Instrument Should I Buy?
- Entry level: Armati ATR213, Blessing XL, Getzen Student 390, Yamaha YTR2335
- Middle level: Bach TR200, Blessing XL, Getzen 590 Capri, Yamaha YTR4335GS
- Upper level: Bach Stradivarius 18043, Blessing Artist ML1, Getzen Eterna 900S, Yamaha YTR6335

Notes on the French Horn

With a long narrow tube coiled into a circular shape before ending in a back-facing bell, the French horn is held with both hands and often rests on the right leg. It commonly has three or four valves. The French horn produces an extensive range of sound. It can play both high and low notes, and the tone is mellow. Musicians play the French horn by tightening and loosening their lips (embouchure) while pressing the valves.

The French horn string (the string that propels valves back and forth) often breaks. Although replacing strings for the first time can be stressful, any parent with a method book, some patience, a straight-edged screwdriver, and some good French horn string can become a repair pro in no time. Just take a deep breath at first, and follow any diagram available in your child's method book. Ask your child's teacher or an instrument repair person if you need some help.

Unique Facts   Complicated technical factors contribute to the difficulty of playing the French horn. Many professional musicians consider it one of the hardest instruments to play.

The French horn originally seems to have developed in France, but it first became popular in Germany. Probably because of its slow valves and smaller sound, few people today actually play the old German horn.

Is the French Horn Right for Us?   Players need teeth that are basically straight, lips that are not large, and hands that are large enough to cover the valves. They also need an unwavering spirit to succeed. The French horn is good for students who don't give up and are attracted to rhythmic, melodic, and technical challenges. Playing the French horn requires an exceptional ear and the ability to distinguish tones quickly and securely. Players should enjoy playing both harmony and melody.

What Supplies Will We Need?   You'll need a soft cleaning cloth, valve oil, a straight mute, a mouthpiece cleaning brush, slide grease, a pencil, extra string for valves, a small flat-edged screwdriver, a method book, and a music stand.

Which Instrument Should I Buy?

- Entry level: Holton H602, Yamaha YHR314
- Middle level: Holton Farkas H181/281, Yamaha YHR567
- Upper level: Conn 11D, Holton H379, Yamaha YHR667VL</bl>

Notes on the Trombone

The simplest in design of all brass instruments, the trombone has a long cylindrical tube bent twice upon itself and opening to a forward-facing flared bell. It has one long, movable U-shaped slide and usually no valves, and its sound is medium low. Musicians play the trombone by tightening and loosening their lips (embouchure) while moving the slide.

The trombone slide is long and if misused will likely become dented and nonfunctional, resulting in tremendous problems for beginning musicians. Encourage your child to *not* dent the slide. Take care of it, and treat it with respect. In addition to weekly applications of slide grease, trombone slides need to be regularly moistened with water. A small spray bottle of water is useful.

Unique Fact   The trombone was the first brass instrument to offer all the notes of the chromatic scale (that's like playing all the black and white keys on a piano). Before the invention of the trombone, note ranges on all brass instruments were limited to the exact size of the instrument.

Is the Trombone Right for Us?   Trombone players need teeth that are basically straight and a medium to large body size with arms long enough to reach out to at least sixth position. They should enjoy playing low notes, harmony, and bass lines.

What Supplies Will We Need?   You'll need a soft cleaning cloth, tuning slide grease, a straight mute, a mouthpiece cleaning brush, a small spray water bottle, a pencil, a method book, and a music stand.

Which Instrument Should I Buy?
- Entry level: Bach Model 16, Conn USA Student Tenor, Blessing B-128, Yamaha YSLTB200925
- Middle level: Bach TB200, Blessing B7/B8, Yamaha YSL400 Series
- Upper level: Bach 42BO, Conn 88H, Blessing B78/B88, Yamaha YSL610/620

Notes on the Baritone Horn/Euphonium and Tuba

All three of these instruments are similar, if not identical, in shape, but they differ mostly in size. All three instruments have either three or four valves. The baritone horn and euphonium are also known as the baby tuba and are about half the size of the regular full-size tuba. Though the baritone horn and euphonium are not identical instruments, their differences are slight and, for our purposes, they will be treated as one instrument.

The longest and lowest instruments in the brass family, all three instruments produce a considerable range of sound, both medium and very low notes. Their tone is deep and rich. Musicians play them by tightening and loosening their lips (embouchure) as they press the valves.

Unique Facts   According to the *Guinness Book of World Records*, Jack Samuel Hogg of the United Kingdom is the oldest tuba player, regularly playing in concerts with the Heswall Concert Band since joining them in 1998 at the age of 94. Jack has been playing a musical instrument since 1919, when as a soprano coronet player he joined the Cammell Laird Sea Scout Band.

Baritone horns and euphoniums are popular in military brass bands. Some of them have bells that are tilted forward instead of upward, making them ideal for marching.

Is the Baritone Horn or Euphonium Right for Us?   Players of these instruments need teeth that are basically straight, medium-size to full lips, and a medium or large body size. They should enjoy deep, warm sounds.

Is the Tuba Right for Us?   The tuba is the largest of the brass family, so a large body size is very helpful. Thick, full lips are ideal, and a large air capacity is important. Players should enjoy low sounds and bass lines.

What Supplies Will We Need? For any of these three instruments, you'll need a soft cleaning cloth, valve oil, a mouthpiece cleaning brush, slide grease, a pencil, a method book, and a music stand.

Which Instrument Should I Buy?

- Entry-level baritone horn/euphonium: Besson BET062, Yamaha YBH301S, Yamaha YEP201
- Middle-level baritone horn/euphonium: Besson 7065, Yamaha YBH621S, Yamaha YEP321
- Upper-level baritone horn/euphonium: Besson 968, Wilson 2704/2900/2950, Yamaha YBH621S, Yamaha YEP642
- Entry-level tuba: Cerveny 471-4, Jupiter 468, Miraphone 182, Yamaha YBB105 3/4
- Middle-level tuba: Cerveny CBB686-R, Miraphone 186, Yamaha YBB3215
- Upper-level tuba: Cerveny ACB601-R, Miraphone 186/191/1291, Yamaha YBB641

MEET THE WOODWIND FAMILY

The woodwind family includes the flute, oboe, bassoon, clarinet, and saxophone. Despite the name, most student-model "woodwind" instruments are *not* made from wood. Instead they are produced with a strong (breakproof and kid-friendly) plastic type of resinate material. All woodwind instruments require air to produce sound. There are three types of woodwind instruments: those that don't require reeds, those with single reeds, and those with double reeds.

Flutes and piccolos do not require reeds. They produce sound when a focused stream of air passes into and over a hole (much like when you blow air over a soft-drink bottle to make a sound). Most woodwind instruments, including clarinets and saxophones, fall into the single-reed category and produce sound with a single reed and a mouthpiece. The reed is held firmly in place against a mouthpiece. Double-reed instruments include the oboe, English horn, and bassoon. They require two reeds that are fastened together.

What Is a Reed?

A reed is a medium-hard, flexible, thinly carved piece of wood or plastic that is set against the mouthpiece of clarinets and saxophones. In the case of oboes and bassoons, reeds are set back to back against each other and tied together, thus the name "double reeds." When air is blown past a reed, it vibrates, resulting in sound. Reeds come in many different densities, shapes, sizes, and varieties. Further, they can be modified by hand to create special sounds or tone colors. Reeds are very delicate and should be handled with care.

Regardless of the care taken, you can expect your child to go through dozens of reeds during the school year, so be sure to purchase several spares to keep on hand. Reeds are not very expensive and are easily replaced. Double reeds do tend to be more expensive than single reeds.

Before playing, your child will need to moisten the reed, as it will "come to life" when wet. Either sucking on it like on a lollipop or placing it in some water for a few minutes will suffice.

Cleaning Woodwind Instruments

Because warm, moist air passes through the plastic, condensation (or "spit") forms on the inside of the instrument. The most common area of condensation buildup is inside of the mouthpiece, between the reed and the mouthpiece. Simply blowing out the unwanted moisture will fix any interference condensation may cause. Additionally, after playing, run a cleaning cloth through the instrument to pull out unwanted moisture. The main concern when cleaning is to reduce or eliminate moisture that causes mold, mildew, and bacteria.

How Often?   Eliminate condensation daily. Thoroughly clean out the mouthpiece at least once a week. Polish and "tune up" the instrument once a month. Have a professional examine the instrument at least once a year, making appropriate pad and key adjustments and checking cork when necessary.

What Do We Need?   You'll need a cleaning cloth, a cleaning swab, a brush, water, soap, key oil, and a soft towel.

How Long Does It Take?   Smaller instruments can be cleaned in about five minutes or less; larger instruments can take upward of fifteen minutes.

What Do We Do?   Eliminate moisture and condensation by swabbing out the instrument after every use. Use a mouthpiece brush to clean out the mouthpiece and to remove unwanted particles from any connecting parts. Also, a cotton swab is useful in cleaning out the hard-to-reach places between keys, pads, holes, and joints. You can also use thin paper, often called cigarette paper, to dry out pads and keyholes. Apply key oil to the movable joints approximately once a month.

Remember that a good-smelling instrument is more fun to play. Encourage your child to brush his or her teeth before playing. This will have a tremendous impact on how the instrument smells.

Notes on the Flute

The flute is a high-pitched cylindrical instrument, usually made from soft metal, with a collection of holes, keys, and pads. Air blowing partly into and partly over the open hole in the mouthpiece, combined with tightening and loosening of the lips, in conjunction with variations in fingering patterns, results in beautiful sound. The piccolo is half the size of the flute and consequently produces a sound twice as high.

Unique Facts   There is considerable solo literature available for the flutist, including songs from hundreds (and thousands) of years ago to songs from current major motion pictures. The flute was a featured solo instrument in the movie *Titanic.*

Flutes seem to have been prevalent in some form or another in nearly every country in the world. It is commonly thought that a long time ago, some ancestral relatives of flutes were made from animal bones!

Is the Flute Right for Us?   Flute players should take pleasure in playing high sounds and melody lines. Students with almost any body type can play the flute.

What Supplies Will We Need?   You'll need two soft cotton towels for cleaning, a pencil, a method book, a music stand, and key oil.

Which Instrument Should I Buy?
- Entry level: Gemeinhardt 2SP, Emerson EM1, Jupiter 313/611, Yamaha YFL221

- Middle level: Gemeinhardt 3S, Emerson EM6SB, Yamaha YFL321
- Upper level: Gemeinhardt 33SB, Emerson EM88/B, Yamaha YFL600 Series

Notes on the Oboe

The oboe is nearly identical in length to the clarinet, and to a casual observer may even look like a clarinet; however, upon careful inspection, there are considerable differences in both shape and sound. Like the clarinet, the oboe extends outward and downward in a straight line when held up to the mouth. It also has a series of keys and holes. The characteristic sound of the oboe is deep and nasal, yet light and sensitive. Many professionals consider the sound uniquely expressive.

Unique Facts   In early classical music, the oboe was the only wind instrument listed on the score; therefore, it is commonly known as the first woodwind instrument in the orchestra. Most professional musicians consider the oboe the most difficult woodwind instrument.

Is the Oboe Right for Us?   Oboe players need an unwavering spirit to succeed and a "get things done correctly" attitude; they need to be people who don't give up. The ideal oboe player is attracted to challenges, enjoys the reed-like sound of the oboe, and likes to play melody lines.

What Supplies Will We Need?   You will need a cleaning swab, at least three extra reeds, a small water container to soak reeds, a music stand, a soft cotton cleaning cloth, a reed case, cork grease, and key oil.

Which Instrument Should I Buy?
- Entry level: Fox 550, Renard 300/400, Selmer Buffet 401, Yamaha YOB241
- Middle level: Buffet 4015/4052, Fox 550/520, Renard 330, Yamaha YOB411
- Upper level: Buffet 3613, Fox 400/450, Yamaha YOB841

Notes on the Bassoon

The bassoon is the natural bass counterpart to the oboe. It is long, is usually made of wood, and has many holes and keys. The bassoon bends downward, and then its main body jets upward with its bell leveling off at or above head level. The bassoon's characteristic sound is low—two octaves lower than an oboe. Like the oboe, it requires a double reed.

Unique Fact The contrabass bassoon is the natural bass to the bassoon. It produces a punchy, loud tone that is twice as low as the bassoon and, in terms of its tone, has been compared to a motorcycle tailpipe.

Is the Bassoon Right for Us? The player's hands must be large enough to cover the proper keys. Bassoonists should enjoy rich and low earthy sounds and bass lines. This challenging instrument is best for a musician with an "I can do it" attitude.

What Supplies Will We Need? You'll need a cleaning swab, a neck or seat strap, three extra reeds, a reed case, a pencil, a soft cleaning cloth, a small water container to soak reeds, cork grease, a music stand, and a method book.

Which Instrument Should I Buy?
- Entry level: Fox Renard Model 41 or Model 51
- Middle level: Schreiber Model S16, Amati Model ABN41S or 81S
- Upper level: Fox Renard Model 240, Selmer Model 132

Notes on the Clarinet

The clarinet family consists of woodwind instruments with mostly straight cylindrical tubes ending with a flaring bell. Most student models are made from molded plastic. All clarinets use single reeds and a mouthpiece and have a series of keys and holes. The characteristic sound of the clarinet is multifaceted because it can play with a rich and full tone, but can also sound vibrant or delicate. Though there are many types of clarinet, three basic sizes with three different sounds are typically used in schools today. The "regular" B-flat clarinet is small and high, the alto clarinet is of medium pitch and size, and the bass clarinet is large and low.

Unique Fact There is considerable solo literature available for the clarinet. Klezmer music often affords many challenging moments for the talented clarinetist.

Is the B-flat Clarinet Right for Us? This clarinet is the smallest of the three basic clarinet types. The player's fingers must be long enough and wide enough to cover the finger holes. The musician should enjoy warm, soft sounds and melody lines.

Is the Alto Clarinet Right for Us?   Body and particularly hand size are a bigger factor in selecting this medium-sized instrument. The musician should enjoy warm, dark sounds.

Is the Bass Clarinet Right for Us?   Body and hand size are most important in selecting this large instrument. Fingers must be able to reach to cover the finger holes in order to produce a tone. A large body type is most appropriate for this instrument. The musician should enjoy playing bass lines.

What Supplies Will We Need?   You'll need a cleaning swab, ten medium-soft reeds, cork grease, a soft cleaning cloth, a reed holder, a pencil, a method book, a music stand, and key oil. Alto and bass clarinetists will also need a neck strap.

Which Instrument Should I Buy?
- Entry-level B-flat clarinet: Buffet B12, Selmer 301, Vito 7214, Yamaha YCL250
- Middle-level B-flat clarinet: Buffet E11, Selmer 211, Vito 7216/7820, Yamaha YCL450
- Upper-level B-flat clarinet: Buffet Prestige R13, Selmer Paris, Yamaha YCL650
- Entry-level alto clarinet: none
- Middle-level alto clarinet: Selmer 1425, Vito 7165, Yamaha YCL230
- Upper-level alto clarinet: Selmer 22-Alto, Yamaha YCL631
- Entry-level bass clarinet: Vito 7166, Yamaha YCL221
- Middle-level bass clarinet: Vito 7166, Yamaha YCL622
- Upper-level bass clarinet: Selmer 35-Bass, Yamaha YCL621

Notes on the Saxophone

The saxophone belongs in the woodwind family even though it is typically made from brass. The saxophone consists of a curved cylindrical tube ending with a flaring bell. It uses single reeds and a mouthpiece and has a series of keys and holes. Its characteristic sound is rich and full. When a saxophone is played with a group of reed instruments, it sounds like a woodwind instrument, but because it is composed primarily of brass, it sounds like a brass instrument if played with brass instruments. Saxophones typically played in schools come in three primary sizes with three correspondingly different sounds. The "regular" alto saxophone is small and high, the tenor saxophone is of medium size and pitch, and the baritone saxophone is large and low.

Unique Fact   Another popular saxophone often featured in music videos and television is called the soprano saxophone. This half-size saxophone plays high notes, but it is not a standard instrument in most school music programs.

Is the Alto Sax Right for Us?   This is the smallest saxophone typically played in schools. The player's fingers must be long enough to reach the keys. The student should enjoy playing high, bright sounds and both harmony and melody lines.

Is the Tenor Sax Right for Us?   Larger hands and fingers and larger body size are helpful in playing this midsize saxophone. The musician should enjoy playing warm sounds and both harmony and melody lines.

Is the Baritone Sax Right for Us?   Because this is the largest saxophone, body size is more important. The player's hands and fingers must cover a wider area than on the other saxophones. The musician should enjoy playing low notes and bass lines.

What Supplies Will We Need?   You'll need a swab, a neck strap, a reed holder, a pencil, a soft cleaning cloth, ten extra reeds, cork grease, a method book, and a music stand.

Which Instrument Should I Buy?
- Entry-level alto sax: Jupiter 767GL, Yamaha YAS23
- Middle-level alto sax: Selmer 230, Yamaha YAS475
- Upper-level alto sax: Selmer Paris Reference 54, Selmer Super Action 62/80, Yamaha YAS6211
- Entry-level tenor sax: Conn Director, Buescher BU5, Yamaha YTS23
- Middle-level tenor sax: Selmer TS200 or La Voix, Vito 7131T/7133T, Yamaha YTS475
- Upper-level tenor sax: Selmer 54 Super Action 80, Yamaha YTS62
- Entry-level baritone sax: Yamaha YBS52
- Middle-level baritone sax: Jupiter 593GL
- Upper-level baritone sax: Jupiter 893SG, Yamaha YBS62, Yanagisawa 901/B991

MEET THE PERCUSSION FAMILY

When we talk about percussion, we refer to many different instruments. Unlike brass, woodwind, and string instruments that are classified by similarities in shape, size, or sound, the snare drum, cymbal, and xylophone have completely different sounds; one is a thump, one is a clang, and the last is a chime. Some percussion instruments tend to make a thud, while others make a ting; still others produce a beautiful melody. Discussion of cleaning and maintaining all percussion instruments is not possible within this book; however, many outstanding guidebooks go into great depth. As with other instruments, common sense and good care habits will prolong the life of any percussion instrument.

Types of Percussion Instruments

I have divided the main percussion instruments into two groups: striking instruments and melodic instruments. Striking instruments, most of which have sound but no clear and discernable tone, make up most of the percussion section. These instruments are usually the first instruments to be taught in a school music program. They include the snare drum, bass drum, cymbal, timpani, and many other auxiliary instruments. Melodic instruments, most of which have a clear and discernable tone, are sometimes overlooked as percussion instruments because they play melodies. These instruments also play harmony and include the xylophone and bells.

Unique Fact   Computers do a great job of simulating the sound of drums; consequently, many rock bands now use computerized drum kits instead of the large drum sets of the past.

Is Percussion Right for Us?   Percussionists should enjoy both rhythmic and melodic challenges and have a never-ending drive and appreciation for rhythm.

What Supplies Will We Need?   You'll need drumsticks of medium strength and size, hard and soft mallets, a bass drum mallet, a carrying case for sticks, a pencil, a drum pad, a method book, two soft cleaning cloths, a music stand, and a drum key.

Which Instrument Should I Buy?
- Entry-level snare drum kit: Yamaha SCK300, Ludwig LE2481, Maypex ED Kit
- Entry-level drum set: Drums in the Wind 5 Piece, Maypex MB5255A
- Middle-level drum set: Maypex Fusion Set, Pearl Export Select, Tama Custom, Yamaha Rydeen
- Upper-level drum set: Ludwig Classic Power Drum, Pearl Stage Pro, Yamaha Pro Series
- Entry-level xylophone/marimba: Musser Student Elite
- Middle-level xylophone/marimba: Musser M61
- Upper-level xylophone/marimba: Musser M51 Pro Portable

MEET THE STRING FAMILY

The string family is made up of four distinct, yet similar, instruments. All four instruments have four strings, pegs, and a main body, but they differ in size, ranging from small to large. All four instruments require a bow. They need to be dusted and polished just like any other instrument, but string instruments have an added issue: because they are made from wood, they are fragile and require delicate handling. Occasionally strings need to be replaced.

String instruments come in different sizes that can accommodate a child's growing body and hands. It is not uncommon to start on a smaller instrument and purchase a more appropriate-sized instrument as your child grows.

Notes on the Violin and Viola

The violin is the smallest instrument in the string family. Its sound is beautiful, enticing, and high. It usually plays melody lines in the orchestra, solo literature, and chamber music. The violin has an extensive collection of solo literature. The viola is nearly identical to the violin in shape, but it is slightly larger and, therefore, produces a slightly lower and deeper sound.

Unique Facts   The violin is also known as the fiddle. Violins produced three hundred years ago by the great maker Stradivarius are cherished for their outstanding, precise, and beautiful sound. There are approximately five hundred Stradivarius violins available in the world, and prices can range well into the tens of thousands of dollars.

Is the Violin Right for Us?   Violinists should take pleasure in playing high sounds and melody lines. Most body types are acceptable.

Is the Viola Right for Us?   Viola players should take pleasure in playing high and medium-high sounds as well as melody and harmony lines. Most body types are acceptable.

What Supplies Will We Need?   You'll need a pencil, a method book, a music stand, rosin, extra strings, and a cleaning cloth.

Which Instrument Should I Buy?
- Entry-level violin: Bellafina 50, Yamaha 7, Florea Persona
- Middle-level violin: Willhelm 2000, Nagoya Suzuki 220
- Upper-level violin: Sophia Prema/Amadeus
- Entry-level viola: Bellafina 50
- Middle-level viola: Bellafina 330, Ren Wei Shi Artist, Willhelm 22
- Upper-level viola: Sophia Amadeus

Notes on the Cello and Bass

The cello is known as the bass member of the string family. Its larger counterpart—the bass (commonly referred to as the double bass)—plays the lowest notes. The cello plays with a luscious, full, and beautiful tone. It has a huge range and is commonly thought of as the premier solo instrument in the orchestra. The bass plays with a deep, dark sound. It typically plays bass lines in the orchestra.

Unique Facts   Many established classical composers have written solo concertos for the cello. Although the cello is larger than the violin, the bow is actually smaller.

Is the Cello Right for Us?   Cellists need to enjoy playing deeper sounds, as well as melody and harmony lines. Larger body types are preferred.

Is the Bass Right for Us?   Bass players should take pleasure in playing low sounds and enjoy playing bass lines and background parts. Larger body types are preferred.

What Supplies Will We Need?   You'll need a pencil, a method book, a music stand, rosin, extra strings, and a cleaning cloth. Bass players will need a special chair.

Which Instrument Should I Buy?
- Entry-level cello: Bellafina 510
- Middle-level cello: Bellafina 535, Ren Wei Shi 7000/8000
- Upper-level cello: Lowis Master Art, Sophia Premium, Yamaha 7
- Entry-level bass: Engelhardt Concert, Strunal 50/1
- Middle-level bass: Engelhardt 5/35
- Upper-level bass: Strunal 5/5WE

· *Appendix D* ·

Annotated Book List

Carlton, Malcolm. *Music in Education: A Guide for Parents and Teachers*. London: Woburn Press, 1989. This book is designed for education majors with little or no background in music. It includes song material and practical instruction on a variety of instruments used in the classroom.

Chroninger, Ruby. *Teach Your Kids about Music: An Activity Handbook for Parents and Teachers Using Children's Literature*. New York: Walker, 1994. This book is aimed at parents, teachers, and caregivers of children from preschool through third grade. It offers suggestions for using children's literature to teach children about rhythm, melody, pitch, tempo, musical instruments, and more.

Cutietta, Robert A. *Raising Musical Kids: A Guide for Parents*. New York: Oxford University Press, 2001. This book provides advice on how to encourage children to appreciate and participate in music. It covers everything from creating a musical home environment and finding a good private teacher to careers in music and community resources.

Exploring Careers in Music. 2nd ed. Reston, Va.: MENC, 2000. This book provides information on a variety of musical careers and the skills and training required to enter them.

Machover, Wilma, and Marienne Uszler. *Sound Choices: Guiding Your Child's Musical Experiences*. New York: Oxford University Press, 1996. This book offers detailed suggestions for choosing an instrument, finding a qualified teacher, and assessing the financial implications of music study. There are also strategies for evaluating the student-teacher relationship, changing teachers, and monitoring practice. A separate section discusses dealing with a musically gifted child or a child with special needs.

Markel, Roberta. *Music for Your Child: A Complete Guide for Parents and Teachers*. New York: Facts on File, 1983. This book includes information on music instruction, matching the instrument to the child, school and community programs, and more.

Music Booster Manual. Reston, Va.: MENC, 1989. This guide to managing a music booster organization covers budgeting, fund-raising, publicity, and gaining community support.

Saperstein, Stella, and Beth Luey. *The Harmonious Child: Every Parent's Guide to Musical Instruments, Teachers, and Lessons.* Berkeley, Calif.: Celestial Arts, 2003. This book covers the basics of finding the right instrument and instructor, music lessons, and managing practice time. It also discusses marching band, orchestra, recitals, and musical careers.

Students' Guide to College Music Programs. Needham, Mass.: Larkin Publications, 2003. This joint publication of Larkin Publications, Hal Leonard, and MENC is designed for students preparing to study music after high school. It includes listings of more than 1,400 colleges and universities and includes information on obtaining financial aid, guidelines for college auditions, and information about careers in the music industry.

About the Author

Tony Bancroft began his instrumental music career at age eleven, playing tuba in middle school band. He continued to pursue his love of music into adulthood, earning a bachelor's degree in music from UCLA and a master's degree in music from Yale University. Performances at Carnegie Hall and at music festivals around the world are among the highlights of his musical career. He currently serves as the music director for the El Segundo Unified School District in California, and the city has honored him with four public commendations. In 2003, he was selected as an alternate for a Fulbright Teaching Scholarship and was a nominee for the Music Center of Los Angeles County's prestigious Bravo Award.